GW00649047

Airway to the East
1918–1920

This book is dedicated to the memory of my father, **Leslie George Semple,** *whose diary, scrapbook and photograph albums were the starting point for my research.*

AIRWAY TO THE EAST 1918–1920

And

The Collapse of No. 1 Aerial Route RAF

by

Clive Semple

Pen & Sword
AVIATION

First published in Great Britain in 2012 by
Pen & Sword Aviation
an imprint of
Pen & Sword Books Ltd
47 Church Street
Barnsley
South Yorkshire
S70 2AS

ISBN: 978-1-84884-657-9

Typeset in 11/13pt Palatino by
Concept, Huddersfield, West Yorkshire

Printed and bound in England by
CPI Group (UK) Ltd, Croydon, CRO 4YY

Pen & Sword Books Ltd incorporates the Imprints of Pen & Sword
Aviation, Pen & Sword Family History, Pen & Sword Maritime, Pen &
Sword Military, Pen & Sword Discovery, Wharncliffe Local History,
Wharncliffe True Crime, Wharncliffe Transport, Pen & Sword Select,
Pen & Sword Military Classics, Leo Cooper, The Praetorian Press,
Remember When, Seaforth Publishing and Frontline Publishing.

For a complete list of Pen & Sword titles please contact
PEN & SWORD BOOKS LIMITED
47 Church Street, Barnsley, South Yorkshire, S70 2AS, England
E-mail: enquiries@pen-and-sword.co.uk
Website: www.pen-and-sword.co.uk

Contents

Acknowledgements

My thanks are mostly due to the successive governments who have maintained the National Archive at Kew at taxpayers' expense. Tucked away in cardboard boxes are the minutes and correspondence of all the ministries for whom records survive. They sometimes reveal well-documented history that conflicts with the traditional version of events that senior politicians and, in this case senior RAF officers, have chosen to present in their semi-official history books. It was the conflict between the truth and these history books that led me to write this account of No. 1 Aerial Route RAF. The first flight to Australia is an integral part of this project so this has also been included in the story.

The Imperial War Museum, The National Archive, the Australian War Memorial and an archive of contemporary photographs from David Hales of a South Australian agency called Optical Design are all to be thanked for supplying most of the pictures. A few were supplied by Chaz Bowyer before he died. The remainder come from my father's photograph albums, were taken by me or are out of copyright.

CHAPTER 1

Bad Landing at Centocelle

It was May 1919. The big Handley Page bomber left Pisa at 5.30 p.m. on the 17th and did not arrive over Centocelle until the light was failing. From the air it is difficult to detect slopes until one is close to them and the pilot, Frederick Prince, misunderstood the landing T and approached downhill. There was no wind and the plane landed too fast. There were no brakes on a Handley Page so it was in danger of overrunning the landing field. Prince switched on his engines again, opened the throttles and tried to go round for a second attempt. As the plane struggled to rise one wing hit a tree and the machine smashed into a road at the edge of the field. Prince was killed outright and Sidney Spratt, his observer and reserve pilot, who was sitting beside him in the nose of the machine, died hours later in hospital.

There was another man sitting in the rear gunner's cockpit and thus protected from the full force of the impact. He was trapped in the wreckage for a time until rescued by the mechanic, Frederick Daw, who had been thrown clear. The other man was T.E. Lawrence, well known and trusted by the Arabs and famous in England as Lawrence of Arabia. Lawrence suffered concussion, a broken collar bone and badly bruised ribs and he was taken to hospital where he remained until the end of May.

While Lawrence was slowly recovering in hospital, Prince and Spratt were buried with full military honours in the St Paolo cemetery for non-Catholics, symbolically located just outside the city walls of Rome. The British Ambassador and the head of the Italian Air Force attended and a firing party from the Italian

1

Centocelle airfield in 1919. Looking down from the air it is not easy to detect the slope of the landing ground. The airfield is now a heavily built-up suburb of Rome inside the ring road. (Air1/2689/15/312/126)

Flying Corps fired a volley over the graves. Only a stone's throw from their graves is the tombstone that marks the spot where the ashes of Percy Bysshe Shelley are interred. Shelley had visited the cemetery not long before he was drowned in 1822 and had written of it:

> The English burying place is a green slope near the walls and is,
> I think, the most beautiful and solemn cemetery I ever beheld.

The remains of the Handley Page D5439 that crashed at Centocelle. It is upside down and only the rear of the fuselage and the tail survived intact. (Chaz Bowyer)

2

To see the sun shining on its bright grass, fresh when we first visited it, with the autumn dews, and hear the whispering of the wind among the leaves of the trees, is to mark the tombs of the mostly young people who are buried there. One might, if one were to die, desire the sleep which they seem to sleep.

See photograph in the colour section.

The two new graves matched Shelley's comment about 'mostly young people'. Frederick Prince was twenty-seven and Sydney Spratt was just nineteen. Ninety years later the crash was remembered by a commemorative service on 19 May 2009 conducted by the Canon of St Mary's Anglican Church in Rome. A handful of Britons attended that service but the rest of Britain knew nothing about it or the reason for the Handley Page being at Rome all those years ago.

Shelley's tombstone. Only his ashes are buried here because his body was burned by Lord Byron and Leigh Hunt on the beach where he drowned in the Gulf of Spezia in 1822. Shelley was returning from a visit to them when his boat was caught in a storm. (CS)

In 1919 few other aeroplanes anywhere in the world had flown as far as this. Those that had were all Handley Pages. Why was a boy of nineteen making a pioneering flight and why was Lawrence there? The answers illuminate a fragment of history that has been concealed for the last ninety years.

Lawrence was on board because he had thumbed a lift to Cairo. He had been attending the Paris Peace Conference as advisor to Prince Feisal, son of the King of the Hejaz,[1] and he was disillusioned by the Machiavellian manoeuvres of the British and French Governments as they tried to take control of the Middle East to fulfil their own post-war strategies.

Lawrence had, in effect, opted out and was returning to Cairo to pick up some papers from the Arab Bureau where he used to work at the beginning of the war. He needed these papers in order to write *The Seven Pillars of Wisdom*, which was his own account of the Arab revolt against the Turks between 1916 and 1918.

Aged twenty-seven, Lieutenant Prince was older and more experienced than most of the other pilots in 58 Squadron RAF. He had been apprenticed into his father's firm of mechanical engineers at Dulwich when he was fifteen. He had already been accepted as an RAF officer with a post-war permanent commission but probably never knew this before he was killed. He later received a posthumous commendation for good work.[2]

Sydney Spratt, who was only nineteen, came from Cheshire. He left school when he was sixteen and worked for his father who was a fruit merchant. He joined the Royal Flying Corps when he was just eighteen and had started his training at Stonehenge for flying the big Handley Pages only six months before he was killed. His personnel record states that he died of injuries so this suggests that he was pulled from the wreckage alive but died soon afterwards.[3] The official record also states that his death occurred 'on the Italian Front'. The War Graves Commission has jumped to the wrong conclusion because the Italian Front was the border between the Austrian and Italian armies in the north of Italy during the war and the war had been over for six months before Spratt was killed. How those in command could sanction such a young and inexperienced boy as second pilot and navigator on a flight like this is beyond understanding today. But in 1919 senior officers, Army or Air Force, had until recently been

The War Graves Commission headstones of Lieutenants Prince and Spratt in St Paolo cemetery, Rome. The design of the lettering on all of the Commission's headstones is standardized but next of kin were allowed to have an inscription of their own choice at the foot of the headstone, as here. (CS)

accustomed to regard the lives of young men as plentiful and cheap.[4]

Lying in bed, Lawrence had time to write notes for his book and to reflect on the chain of events that had led to this narrow escape. It was by no means his first. His career had been one long hair-raising adventure ever since he undertook an 1,100-mile walking tour of Syria and Palestine in 1909 as an undergraduate, sketching Crusader castles and studying their architecture. This is where the career began that made him famous and it is also the beginning of a chain of events that led to a foolhardy project, to fly fifty-one bombers to Cairo in 1919 when neither the machines nor the pilots were capable of doing it. The story remains unknown to the public because it was deliberately suppressed by senior Army and Air Force officers at the time. As far as the author knows this is the first time that the suppressed events have seen the full light of day, although accounts of them are tucked away in files held in the National Archive at Kew and they have been available to serious historians for many years.

Notes

1. The Hejaz is now western Saudi Arabia.
2. Frederick George Prince. 47 Rosendale Road, Dulwich, London SE 21. Born 17.7.1891.
3. Sydney Spratt. 217 Seaview Road, Wallasey, Cheshire. Born 3.11.99.
4. I have told the War Graves Commission of their mistake but they prefer to stick with their own story.

CHAPTER 2

The Army and the Navy Disagree

Lawrence's encounter with the Handley Page O/400 bomber on his trip to Rome in 1919 was not the first time that he had met this remarkable aeroplane. Even today, only aviation historians know that such large aeroplanes flew as early as this. They were as big as the Flying Fortress of World War Two and could carry twenty-three people or more than a ton of bombs. They first came into service in 1917 and were the most powerful machines of any nation to take part in World War One. More than 550 were built and in 1918 100 sets of components were despatched to the USA for assembly there although only seven of these had been built before the war ended so quickly and unexpectedly. Sadly, not a single one survives, not even in a museum. Since forty-five of the fifty-one bombers that tried to fly to Cairo were of this type it is worthwhile saying a little more about them.

This aeroplane's creation was largely due to the far-sightedness of a handful of people in the Royal Navy, strongly supported by the First Lord of the Admiralty, Winston Churchill.

On 1 July 1914, the Naval Wing of the Royal Flying Corps broke away from the Military Wing and unilaterally declared itself as the Royal Naval Air Service, directly under Admiralty command. The Navy had different ideas from the Army about the future of aviation and there was friction between the two Services. The Army saw aeroplanes principally as an aid to front-line troops,

A Handley Page O/400 at Cranwell in early 1918. Beside it for comparison is a Sopwith Camel. The man whose head is almost touching one blade of a propeller is my father who was training as a Handley Page pilot at the time. (LGS)

carrying out reconnaissance and attacking railways, roads and airfields in the forward area. For this, low-powered, two-seat, short-range machines were needed. The Navy saw aviation as a means of attacking more distant targets such as factories, docks, Zeppelin hangars and ships. For this it wanted aeroplanes with a range of several hundred miles that could carry a worthwhile load of bombs or torpedoes.

When the war began the Superintendent of Aircraft Design at the Admiralty was Commander Murray Sueter. Churchill was an aviation enthusiast and at his request Sueter went to see Frederick Handley Page and his Chief Designer, George Volkert, at the Handley Page aircraft factory at Cricklewood. Sueter explained what he wanted but Handley Page failed to grasp the full meaning of Commander Sueter's request. 'Look Mr Page,' said Sueter. 'What I want is a bloody paralyser of an aeroplane, to stop the Hun in his tracks.'[1]

The task faced by George Volkert and his design team was daunting. The plane had to carry six 100-pound bombs and fly four hundred miles without refuelling. Nothing like this had been attempted before. It would weigh twice as much as any machine built so far and have a wingspan of 100 feet.

The first prototype was built at the Cricklewood factory and assembled in another factory at Kingsbury. From there it was towed, late at night, along the Edgeware Road and down Colindale

8

Churchill as a would-be pilot in 1913. (Chaz Bowyer)

Avenue to the aerodrome at Hendon, which the RNAS had commandeered from its flying school owners in 1914. Because of its 100-foot wingspan it was named the Handley Page O/100. It was much the largest aeroplane seen so far and lamp posts, overhead tram wires and telephone lines had to be removed and trees cut down to get it there. Local residents protested at the damage but the Defence of the Realm Act brooked no opposition. The Government could do anything it liked if it helped the war effort. Later a new factory and an aerodrome were laid out at Cricklewood. The machine made its first flight on 17 December 1915. Since it was constructed of wood, canvas and wire with a few metal struts it was just as vulnerable to the weather as the smaller machines and between flights it was housed with its wings folded in a canvas Bessonneau hangar. The hangar had to be raised on packing cases to make it high enough. On occasions when no tractor was available, the aeroplane needed forty men to manhandle it.

Four prototypes were built with successive changes in design and eventually the Handley Page O/100 went into production and a few saw active service under Admiralty control in France. By the middle of 1917 the Navy's ambitions had grown. It was demanding a 2,000-pound bomb load and yet greater range.

Handley Page fitted more powerful engines and made improvements to the arrangement and capacity of the petrol tanks. The new model was designated O/400. By the end of the war they were being built in eleven different factories in Britain as well as in the USA.

The Handley Pages were designed as night bombers and equipped with two machine gunners as well as a pilot, a navigator/second pilot and a worthwhile load of bombs. Because they flew at night they were rarely attacked by fighters but they had searchlights, anti-aircraft guns, engine failures and navigation errors to contend with. As the Handley Page bombers began to pour out of the factories they were sent to France and most of them were used in tactical support of the Army. The Navy wanted to use them to attack German industrial sites but Field Marshal Haig was in charge and nobody, not even the Prime Minister, Lloyd George, dared gainsay him. Haig, as well as being a dominant personality, had married one of the ladies in waiting to Queen Alexandra and this gave him unrivalled personal and private access to her son King George V who still had great influence on government policy.

By the time the war ended in November 1918 there were eight squadrons of Handley Pages based in northern France. Each

The first prototype Handley Page O/100 at Hendon in December 1915. Note that it had an enclosed cockpit, which was later removed at the pilots' request. Up to this time all aeroplanes had open cockpits and the pilots thought that enclosure would spoil visibility. Since they typically flew at 70mph the wind was no problem. On later models the nose of the machine was lengthened,which further improved side-to-side visibility. (Chaz Bowyer)

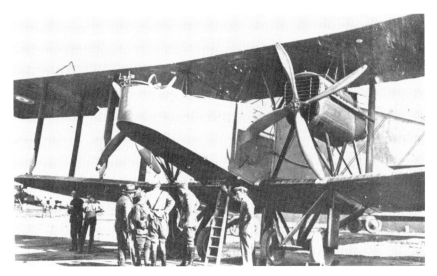

Winston Churchill (in trilby hat) inspecting an early HP O/400. (Chaz Bowyer)

squadron had ten bombers in active service with several more in reserve. Most had been used on short-range attacks on railways and airfields while a few made longer-range attacks on industrial targets across the Rhine. More machines were waiting in England but with the war over, apart from airmail runs to the Army of Occupation, there was little for them to do.

By the spring of 1919 the situation was changing. As the war in Europe came to an end another war began in the Middle East – a war for which Britain and France were, initially, largely responsible and which continues to this day but with the USA, Israel, Palestine and its growing number of Muslim supporters as the principal protagonists. To understand how this came about we have to understand British attempts to unseat the Turks in the Middle East during World War One.

Note
1. The origin of the phrase 'bloody paralyser' is disputed but this version is the best.

Chapter 3

Desert Revolt and the Allenby Campaign

Until 1917 the Turks, allies of Austria and Germany in the Great War, controlled most of the Middle East. Theoretically, Egypt was also part of this Ottoman Empire but corruption and incompetence had fatally weakened it. Britain had taken military control of Egypt in 1882 in order to protect the Suez Canal. By the outbreak of war in 1914 Egypt was de facto a British Protectorate with a sultan chosen and appointed by the British.

Before the outbreak of war the Turks allowed the Germans to train their army and to construct railways from Baghdad and Damascus 900 miles south to Medina in the heartland of the Hejaz. These railways were the lifeline for the Turkish garrisons scattered through Syria, Palestine and Arabia. It was clear that when war began Turkey would side with Germany. So Sherif Hussein of Mecca, the ruler of the Hejaz and a descendant of Mohammed, but still a subject and unwilling tax payer of the Ottoman Empire, saw an opportunity to throw off the Turkish yoke by allying himself with Britain, which already controlled the nominally Ottoman province of Egypt.

Since the Turks were committed to the Germans, it was in Britain's interest to encourage the Arabs within the ailing Ottoman Empire to revolt against their Turkish overlords. Despite being fellow Muslims, the Arabs were becoming increasingly restive and nationalist. Turks may be Muslims but racially they are not Arabs and racial differences can prove as divisive as religious ones.

A two-year negotiation took place between Sir Henry McMahon, the British High Commissioner in Egypt and Sherif Hussein. The Arabs agreed to revolt against the Turks in return for a promise from Britain that they would be rewarded with independence in all the freed territories when the war ended. With small exceptions in the Lebanon, Jerusalem, Baghdad and Basra, the British Government agreed to this in writing. The details of this agreement may be seen in The National Archive at Kew.[1] See coloured map.

Matters were brought to a head in May 1916 when twenty-one Arab nationalists were arrested by the Turks in Damascus and hanged in public. A month later the Arab revolt began in Hussein's heartland, Medina. It was led by Prince Feisal whose father Sherif Hussein rode to Mecca and fired a symbolic shot at the Turkish barracks there. Since he had been born in 1854 he was too old to take an active part in the revolt himself and he left leadership of the fighting to his sons, Ali, Feisal, Abdullah and Zeid. During the rest of 1916 the Arabs made piecemeal progress along the coast of the Red Sea, freeing the towns of the Hejaz from the Turks. From time to time they were aided by bombardments from the French and British navies in the Red Sea and they were supplied with food from India by the same route. The Royal Navy's assistance included the early use of a ship as an aircraft carrier. It was a converted Isle of Man ferry.

HMS *Ben My Chree*. The name means 'Girl of my Heart' in Manx. (IWM SP494)

As can be seen in the photo, a hangar was built behind the funnels, which housed six seaplanes, and the arms of a winch can be seen in the stern. A seaplane was winched over the side of the ship and it took off from the water for bombing or reconnaissance work. When its mission was finished it landed on the sea and taxied back to its mother ship where it was winched aboard and pushed back into the hangar. In calm seas the system worked well and the carrier assisted in the destruction of the fortifications at Jeddah, close to Mecca, one of the first Red Sea ports to be captured from the Turks during the Arab revolt.

When the Revolt began it was entirely an Arab affair and the Arabs rejected help from the French or British armies because they were Christian and were therefore forbidden to go anywhere near the Holy places at Medina and Mecca. It remained an exclusively Arab campaign until the autumn of 1916 when T.E. Lawrence came on the scene. He played a significant role, although perhaps not as significant as he would have us believe in his *Seven Pillars of Wisdom*. Lawrence was concerned about writing good prose rather than good history and he said himself that some fiction was needed to make a good story.

While working as a Middle Eastern archaeologist in 1913 he had learned Arabic and several of its dialects. His understanding of it was patchy but it was better than that of most British diplomats. He had also acquired an understanding of Arab culture that was rare for an Englishman of that time. With these qualifications he was drafted into the War Office, at the age of only twenty-five, and sent in 1914 to the Army Intelligence Service in Cairo, which monitored Arab opinion and helped plan British military strategy. These responsibilities soon broadened into moulding Arab opinion towards British interests and against those of the Turks. The office to which he was sent later became known as the Arab Bureau.

By the autumn of 1916 the Arab campaign was faltering. Many of the tribesmen went home to help with the harvest or simply to renew acquaintance with their wives and there was not enough loot to keep them interested. So in October 1916 Lawrence was sent from the Arab Bureau in Cairo to work with them. The rest of the staff at the Arab Bureau breathed a sigh of relief because he did not 'fit in' in military circles. He was careless in dress and despised upper class protocol. The fact that he and his siblings were illegitimate may account for some of his anti-establishment attitude. But he quickly became accepted as one of the leaders of the rebellion. He disguised his Christian culture by dressing in Arab clothes and by being at pains to eat and sleep like the Bedouin Arabs around him.

Today we can appreciate that the success of the rebellion was largely due to the guerrilla tactics of Lawrence and the Arabs who wisely avoided pitched battles and pinned down thousands of regular army Turks with handfuls of their own men. This was of real assistance to the British Army who were defending the Suez Canal and short of men because of the needs of the Western Front. The Turks soon learned that regular armies have little success against adequately funded guerrillas. The lesson has not yet sunk in with the armies of the West.

Lawrence lived like the Bedouin. He took the same risks as those who fought with him and was an inspiration to others as well as proving himself as a strategist. Arab military effectiveness was sadly hampered by inter-tribal rivalries and Lawrence acted skilfully as arbiter when disputes arose. On one occasion he was obliged to judge, shoot and kill a headstrong Arab who had killed someone else in an argument. Only Lawrence could do it other-wise a tribal feud would have developed. He managed to maintain a fighting force even though some Bedouin tribes came and went as the mood took them. Their mood was improved from time to time by gold, food, rifles and ammunition supplied by the British High Commissioner in Cairo.[2] The Arab's main leader was Prince Feisal whom Lawrence had decided was the most promising of Sherif Hussein's sons but Abdullah, Ali, Zeid and many other tribal leaders played prominent roles in the campaign.

Sadly, Britain never had any intention of honouring the agreement that Sir James McMahon had reached with Sherif Hussein in October 1915 about future independence for the Arabs. While McMahon was negotiating with Sherif Hussein, a French diplomat called M. Georges-Picot and an English diplomat called Sir Mark Sykes were making an agreement as to how Britain and France would share out the spoils of victory in the Middle East when the war was over. (Sir Mark Sykes is not to be confused with Sir Frederick Sykes who appears later in the book.)

France was to have Syria, the Lebanon, northern Mesopotamia and some influence in Jerusalem. Britain was to have the rest of

Sherif Hussein

Lawrence

Lawrence (standing) with his bodyguard in 1917. To the Arabs he was 'El Aurens'. (Q59576)

Mesopotamia and Palestine. Only Jordan, the Yemen and what we now call Saudi Arabia, were to be left under Arab control. See map in the colour section. This agreement was signed in May 1916 but was kept secret at the time to avoid upsetting the Arabs. However, since Russia was an ally, the Czarist government was kept informed. The Arabs did not get to hear of it until after the Russian revolution when the Bolsheviks leaked the story to Sherif Hussein.

The fact that the Sykes-Picot Agreement completely cut across the McMahon-Hussein Agreement signed in October 1915 did not worry the British Government at the time. The war in France was going badly for the Allies and any help the Arabs could give by

M. Georges-Picot

Sir Mark Sykes

17

harassing the Turks in the Middle East was welcome. The longer-term implications of making an agreement with the Arabs that Britain had no intention of honouring were ignored. After all the Arabs were weak, disorganized, poorly armed and not educated enough to form an effective government. The future would take care of itself under British and French control. Or so it seemed at the time.

In July 1917, after an epic 600-mile ride across the desert, the Arabs charged the town of Aqaba from the landward side and captured it. They took the Turks by surprise because the Turks regarded the route taken by the Arabs as impossible because it was waterless. On this journey to Aqaba Lawrence and Feisal began with less than 100 men. For several days they were in the saddle for twenty-two hours a day with a handful of them taking it in turn to lead through the darkness.

As they approached Aqaba the local tribesmen, through whose lands they passed, began to take an interest in the prospect of the capture of this well supplied town and they joined the final charge in their hundreds in order to qualify for a share in the Turkish loot.

The flag designed by Sir Mark Sykes for the Arab revolt. He was the British diplomat who later betrayed the Arabs by making a secret agreement with M. Georges-Picot of France that contradicted what Sir James McMahon had agreed with Sherif Hussein. (T.E. Lawrence)

Feisal's army entering Yenbo in December 1916. (Q58754)

Meanwhile, the British Army in Egypt was also active. British possessions in India and the Far East made control of the Suez Canal vital. During the war the Turks made two attempts to capture or destroy it but both were unsuccessful. The allied army in Egypt was greatly expanded and became known as the Egyptian Expeditionary Force. As aviation developed the Royal Flying Corps established an airbase and pilot training facilities at Heliopolis, just north of Cairo. The Royal Flying Corps (RFC) also established bases at Aboukir, on the Nile Delta, and at Ismailia, halfway down the Suez Canal. The Air Officer Commanding in the Middle East was Brigadier Geoffrey Salmond. His deputy,

Drawing water at a well, April 1917. (Q58949)

19

who arrived in January 1917, was Lieutenant Colonel Amyas Borton, known affectionately to his friends as 'Biffy'. These men are two more links in the chain of events described in this book.

Aqaba was the northernmost port on the Red Sea and brought the Arabs to within 150 miles of Suez. This enabled Lawrence to make the journey by camel from Aqaba to Cairo to make contact with the Expeditionary Force making its way from the Suez Canal to the Palestine border.

Aqaba became the headquarters of the Arab army for the next year because it could be supplied from the Red Sea and because Lawrence could make contact with the British forces in Egypt by ship, camel or aeroplane. Thereafter the Expeditionary Force and the Arabs worked together in a twin-pronged attack on the Turks with the Expeditionary Force advancing up the Palestinian and Syrian coast and the Arabs advancing inland across Sinai and up through Jordan towards Syria.

By the time of Aqaba's capture the war was safely distant from the Muslim Holy Places and Sherif Hussein had no objection to a handful of British advisors joining the Arab forces. The leader of this group of twelve was a Royal Engineers officer, Lieutenant Colonel Stewart Newcombe, who had been with Lawrence during the excavations at Carchemish in 1913. He taught the Arabs how to use explosives – a skill they have exploited ever since.

The advance on Aqaba, July 1917. (Q59193)

HMS *Humber* at Aqaba. (Q59064)

The Egyptian Expeditionary Force consisted of British, Indian, Australian and New Zealand troops and this brings us to the Australian link in this story. The previous year had seen the slaughter of a million French and British soldiers on the Somme and at Verdun. Loyal soldiers from Australia and New Zealand flocked to Britain's aid. But instead of going to the Western Front as they expected, they were disembarked in Egypt and sent to Gallipoli. After the disastrous Dardanelles campaign in which 10,000 ANZACs (Australian and New Zealand Army Corps) were killed and 25,000 injured, the surviving ANZAC forces were withdrawn to Egypt. Most of the Australian Imperial Force eventually moved on to France but the Australian Light Horse and the New Zealand Mounted Rifles remained in Egypt with the Expeditionary Force.

In August 1914 a twenty-three-year-old lad from Adelaide had enlisted in the 3rd Regiment of the Australian Light Horse. As the son of a sheep farmer he was a good horseman and part of his education had been at his father's old school at Moffat in Scotland so he had strong feelings of loyalty towards the mother country. He was quickly promoted to sergeant and on 22 October embarked for Egypt. His dismounted regiment landed at Gallipoli in May 1915. He was promoted to sergeant major in August and commissioned in September. He was wounded and invalided to England but returned to Egypt in May 1916. Back in his regiment in August he took part in the Battle of Romani, which was the final

Lieutenant Colonel Stewart Newcombe RE. (Q58908)

Turkish attempt to seize the Suez Canal. During this battle the twenty-five-year-old led a machine gun battery. The allied forces were commanded by an Australian, Major General Chauvel, and it was the first battle in World War One on any front in which the

Blowing up the Hejaz railway. (Q58704)

Allies achieved a decisive victory. Thereafter, the Expeditionary Force slowly advanced towards the Egyptian frontier and ultimately all the way to Damascus. See the colour photo of the Australian Light Horse. The name of the boy from Adelaide was Ross Smith and he figures prominently in this book.

In response to a British appeal, Australia formed the nucleus of an Australian Flying Corps (AFC) in 1916. This nucleus was named No. 1 Squadron AFC and moved to Egypt in April where it became part of No. 5 Wing of the Royal Flying Corps. The pilots and aircrew were trained by RFC personnel at Heliopolis and Brigadier Geoffrey Salmond was delighted with them.

> The rapid training and mobilization of the Squadron reflected great credit on the industry, keenness and discipline of all ranks.[3]

No. 1 Squadron first went into action on 30 October 1916 when it raided Beersheba, the Turkish Army Headquarters and site of the principal German aerodrome.

Both sides had aircraft and they were particularly useful for reconnaissance because it was impossible to hide from them in the desert. The weather was nearly always reliable and there were frequent dogfights as each side tried to prevent the other from seeing their troop movements. Aeroplanes were also useful for making photographic maps. There were few other maps available for these remote areas. It was decided to expand the AFC in Egypt to four squadrons and volunteers from Australian Army units in Egypt were sought. Lieutenant Ross Smith volunteered in July 1917 and easily qualified. It was found that good horsemen usually made good pilots and Ross was no exception.

In early 1917 RFC aeroplanes in Egypt were no match for the Germans. In line with War Office policy, the RFC had concentrated on the development of easy-to-fly two-seat reconnaissance machines such as the Be2c. They were easy to fly because they were stable. My father learned to fly the Be2c at Cranwell in 1917 and, according to his diary, was delighted with it.[4] The pilot could take his hands and feet off the controls and it would fly by itself. This made it ideal for reconnaissance because hands could be devoted to photography and mapping. But this very stability

Map from Arthur Banks – *A Military Atlas of the First World War.*

was its undoing. It was stable because it was slow to respond to the controls and with a high-performance German fighter in pursuit that was disastrous. The Germans had Halberstadts and Fokkers in Egypt with machine guns synchronized to fire through their propellers. It was claimed that the skill of the British and Australian pilots compensated for the inferiority of their machines but that was only propaganda and the Germans had air superiority in both France and the Middle East during most of 1917. The Be machines were gradually retired from the Western Front but the RFC had eight squadrons of them in the Middle East.

The situation changed in late 1917 with the arrival of the latest British fighter, the Bristol F2b, which was developed by private enterprise under contract to the Royal Naval Air Service. The Bristols had synchronized forward-firing Vickers machine guns just like the Fokkers. But unlike the Fokkers they also had powerful Rolls-Royce engines and Lewis machine guns mounted in a rear cockpit with an all-round firing capability. Their arrival in the Middle East changed the balance of power in the air in Britain's favour and Ross Smith was one of the first pilots to fly them.

The Be aircraft continued to do the aerial photography, mapping and tracking of enemy movements, but now they were escorted by the Bristols. The Fokkers kept out of the way and Turkish and German aerial reconnaissance was greatly reduced on Allenby's

No. 1 Squadron AFC planes housed in their primitive hangars in the desert.
(Q59032)

The elegant-looking but vulnerable Be2c.

front. Without it the German commander, General Liman von Sanders, could not tell where the next attack might come from. An official German war diary for June 1918, captured when Nablus was taken, recorded:

> The enemy, who possesses in his Bristol fighter an exceptionally fine machine has made himself lately very redoubtable. Nearly always flying in twos, the Bristol fighters present an extraordinary fighting force and their harassing of our activities becomes more and more felt.

The Fokker Eindecker with its forward-firing synchronized machine gun.

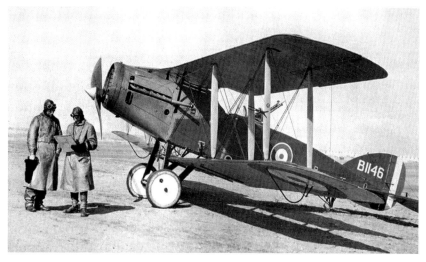

Ross Smith (left) with a Bristol F2b fighter in Palestine. (AWM P03631.013)

There were occasions when flights of five of the German Fokkers encountered pairs of Bristols. The Fokkers usually avoided action and fled. Shortly after arriving at their new base at Ramleh, two Bristols, piloted by Tonkin and Ross Smith, encountered a

Captain Ross Smith and his gunner Lieutenant Mustard in a Bristol F2b with twin Lewis machine guns. (AWM A00658)

German Rumpler, which they shot down. They also encountered two Albatros scouts, which they forced down.

Ross Smith became a skilled pilot and was awarded the Military Cross twice and the Distinguished Flying Cross three times. Altogether, he shot down nine German or Turkish planes. This naturally brought him to the attention of senior RFC officers and one of these was that other link in the chain of events, Lieutenant Colonel Amyas Borton who was commander of No. 5 Wing RFC, to which No.1 Squadron belonged. Smith and Borton had something in common, both had been shot in aerial dogfights and both had brought their machines safely back to base afterwards. Smith's face had been grazed by a bullet in a skirmish over Beersheba in 1917 and Borton had suffered a bullet through the jaw. For bringing his machine and his observer safely back to base after this incident he and his observer were awarded the DSO. The citation in the *London Gazette* on 3 July 1915 reads:

> When on flying reconnaissance over the neighbourhood of Staden on 7th June 1915, Captain Borton was wounded in the head and neck by a bullet fired from a hostile aeroplane, and although suffering severely from loss of blood he continued, with the assistance of the Observer, Captain Marshall, to bandage his wounds and completed the reconnaissance on the prescribed course. His injuries are such that he is not yet out of danger. Captain Marshall continued his observations after rendering all possible aid to the pilot, who was gradually losing consciousness, notwithstanding that the German aeroplane was persistently attacking. The valuable report supplied by this officer is as detailed and complete for the last as it is for the first part of the reconnaissance.

Biffy Borton began the war as a Black Watch officer. He came from a brave Edwardian family with an empire-building background and he usually wore a monocle. He learned to fly in 1912 and when war broke out he transferred to the RFC as a pilot in No. 5 Squadron. He was promoted captain in June 1915 and appointed squadron commander (or major) of No. 27 Squadron in France. In January 1917 he was posted to Palestine as wing commander (Lieutenant Colonel) of No. 5 Wing RFC.

Lieutenant Colonel Amyas Borton RFC   Captain Ross Smith AFC

Meanwhile, 1917 had seen a profound change in the political situation. The Russian revolution had brought about the collapse of the Czarist armies and the United States had joined the war in April. At this time the American Army comprised 6,000 officers and 122,000 men. Conscription was introduced on 18 May but it

Ross Smith (left) with Amyas Borton, standing beside a German machine that Smith had just shot down. (IWM HU57897)

took another year before American troops were ready for action. During that year some further encouragement from Britain was needed to bring these troops to France. Jewish influence on the British Cabinet and in both Houses of Congress was strong and, on 2 November, Britain, with the Balfour Declaration, advocated the establishment of a national home for the Jews in Palestine.[5] At that time Israel did not exist and only 7 per cent of the Palestinian population was Jewish. The Balfour Declaration contained a proviso that the interests of the existing population of Palestine should be protected. That promise was not honoured and much suffering has resulted.

In June 1917 General Sir Edmund Allenby took over from General Sir Archibald Murray as commander of the Egyptian Expeditionary Force. Allenby was a hard and determined man. He was not loved but he was respected and he set the tone for his leadership by moving his headquarters up to the front line, whereas his predecessor, Sir Archibald Murray, had been content to run the war from his headquarters in Cairo. Murray had, nevertheless, built a railway and a water pipeline all the way from Suez to the border near Gaza. This was essential before the advance into Palestine could begin. The Expeditionary Force advanced up the coast through Gaza and on towards Jaffa while Prince Feisal and the Arabs, with Lawrence and a handful of British in support, advanced inland. As the British soldiers entered Jerusalem on 9 December, they were greeted with joy by Jews and Arabs alike. Both were delighted to be rid of the Turks and both thought that Britain would safeguard their interests in Palestine.

In Britain, *Punch* magazine, which was always quick to celebrate British victories in the Great War, real or imaginary, published a full page cartoon about it in December 1917.

The cartoon celebrating the capture of Jerusalem was, by today's standards, politically inept. It displayed no thought for the Muslim point of view but it was probably popular in Britain, just like Sir Hubert Parry's choral work 'Jerusalem', which appeared at much the same time. General Allenby was a better diplomat than the editor of *Punch* and he appreciated Arab sensitivity to the 'conquest' of Jerusalem by a Christian army. He made sure of a welcome as a liberator rather than a conqueror by dismounting from his horse outside the city and entering it on foot, accompanied by Lawrence.

The Punch cartoon Richard, Coeur de Lion looking down on the Holy City. 'At last my dream comes true!'

General Allenby arriving at the Jaffa Gate of Jerusalem on 11 December 1917. (Q51387)

Lloyd George displayed no more diplomatic wisdom than the editor of *Punch* in gloating over the capture of Jerusalem. Indeed, it looks as though he took his cue from the *Punch* cartoon. Ten days after Jerusalem was taken by Allenby, he told the House of Commons:

> The capture of Jerusalem has made a most profound impression throughout the whole civilized world. The most famous city in the world after centuries of strife and vain struggle … has fallen into the hands of the British Army, never to be restored to those who successfully held it against the embattled hosts of Christendom … I venture to say that the achievements of British troops in Mesopotamia and Palestine which have been the cradle and shrine of civilization, will remain for many ages to come.

General Allenby dismounted when he reached the Jaffa Gate and entered Jerusalem on foot. Walking with him was T.E. Lawrence. (T.E. Lawrence)

The German and Turkish retreat continued until they reached a natural defensive position in the Nablus hills and there was a lull in Allenby's campaign after the capture of Jerusalem. No British reinforcements were available because of the critical nature of the war on the Western Front where the German spring 1918 offensive had begun. Not dependent on regular army support, the Arabs continued their steady advance through Sinai and into Jordan, although they lacked the air support that Allenby's troops enjoyed.

The Australian Flying Corps squadrons moved up to Ramleh, between Jaffa and Jerusalem and by March 1918 No. 1 Squadron was fully equipped with eighteen Bristol F2b aircraft. During the lull in the fighting, the Australian squadrons carried out a major mapping survey again using the Bristol fighters as an escort for the Be2cs. Reconnaissance east of the Dead Sea showed Turkish preparations for defence indicating that the Hejaz Arabs were coming nearer.

Once again Biffy Borton congratulated the four squadrons of Australians on their work and he too received credit for their achievements. He became a full colonel in November 1917 and a brigadier on 1 April 1918, the day on which the Royal Air Force was officially created. Thereafter the RFC was replaced by the RAF, although army ranks continued in the RAF until August 1919.

No. 1 Squadron Australian Flying Corps.

Notes

1. Sir Henry McMahon – Correspondence between Sir Henry McMahon and Sherif Hussein of Mecca. HMSO Cmd.5957. London. 1939. PRO fiche 147.289.
2. The gold came as sackfuls of sovereigns, minted in Australia.
3. F.M. Cutlack, *The Australian Flying Corps in the 1914–18 War*. Naval & Military Press.
4. See my previous book *Diary of a Night Bomber Pilot*, p. 96.
5. The story of the development of Zionism in Britain in which Churchill played a large and, for him, profitable part, is much more complex than this reference to it suggests. It is a controversial subject that needs a book of its own, but not the one by Martin Gilbert a Jewish Zionist who is biased in Churchill's favour.

CHAPTER 4

Borton's Pioneering Flight

In June 1918, during the temporary lull in fighting in Palestine, caused by the shortage of British reinforcements, Brigadier Borton was able to come home to Kent for three weeks leave. After his leave, which he spent with his parents at Cheveney in Kent, he was granted an extra ten days to familiarize himself with advances in aviation that had been made since he went to the Middle East in January 1917. He visited various squadrons in England and saw the new Handley Page O/400s in action. He was greatly impressed and proposed to the Air Ministry in London that he should be allowed to fly one out to Egypt. It would be useful for bombing in Allenby's campaign where there was nothing like it and it would also test the feasibility of long-distance air routes when the war was over.

A twin-engined Handley Page O/100 bomber had already been flown from Britain to Lemnos in the Aegean as long ago as May 1917. The flight took fifteen days but involved over-sea flying of only about 100 miles. On 9 July 1917, this machine flew from the Royal Naval Air Service base on the island of Lemnos in the Aegean to Constantinople and bombed the German cruisers *Goeben* and *Breslau*, lying at the Golden Horn. The crew of the Handley Page claimed four direct hits on *Goeben* and more on the Turkish War Office nearby.[1] The flight from England was the first route of more than 2,000 miles that had been flown anywhere in the world and, combined with news of the attack in Constantinople harbour, it made headlines. Squadron Commander Savory received a bar to his DSO and Flight Lieutenant MacLelland and Lieutenant

Rawlings received DSCs. The two mechanics were awarded DSMs. There was a long report in the *Daily Express* on 14 December about the flight from England to the Aegean. So low was the plane as it crossed the Albanian mountains that they saw horsemen only a stone's throw below chasing them in the hope of a forced landing. Fortunately, the horsemen had no rifles and the aeroplane did not have to land.[2]

While the Air Ministry was considering Brigadier Borton's proposal he went over to France and visited Handley Page squadrons that were in action there. When he returned he found that his request to fly one to Egypt had been accepted by the Chief of the Air Staff (CAS), Major General Sir Frederick Sykes, and Borton was sent to Cranwell to familiarize himself with the new aeroplane and learn to fly it. He was to be accompanied by Major Stuart McLaren, who was already a Handley Page pilot, and two mechanics.

Before the flight could begin, a lot of planning was needed. The range of a Handley Page O/400 was a maximum of about 600 miles and could be much less with a strong headwind, so a chain of refuelling and maintenance bases had to be prepared. The route would be mostly overland. France and Italy were both allies of Britain and by 1918 both countries had large air forces and suitable airfields all the way across France and down to the toe of Italy.

As Turkey, Syria and most of Palestine were still enemy territory, the later stages of the route would have to be across the Mediterranean. This meant establishing a refuelling base on Crete or Malta. Neither of these islands at this stage had any airfields. Of the two, Crete was preferred because the nearest African landfall was at Sollum, much nearer Cairo than Benghazi, which was the nearest landfall on the Malta route. The British administration in Cairo had already built a coastal road to Mersah Matruh and Sollum and both towns had British garrisons. But the desert further west towards Benghazi was sparsely occupied by bloodthirsty Senussi tribesmen. Encouraged and bribed by the Turks, they had revolted against the Allies in November 1915 and Britain, France and Italy had been obliged to keep 110,000 troops in North Africa for most of the war.

The route chosen by Borton was subsequently drawn and coloured on a pretty map, which is now filed away in The National

Archive. It is reproduced in the colour page section of this book. It was designated as No. 1 Aerial Route, RAF. There never was another official 'Aerial Route'. In books on the history of the RAF the *next* leg of the journey from Cairo to India is generally referred to as the 'first aerial route', perhaps to obscure memories of the real No. 1 Aerial Route. Most RAF historians are retired senior RAF officers and they seem unwilling to admit that the official No. 1 Aerial Route ever existed. Military history can be very selective when it is written by military men.

A landing ground and refuelling station at Sollum on the Libyan coast was no problem. RAF fighters had already found and used a fortuitously flat area of hard sand on the Mediterranean shore as a refuelling point. There was also a lagoon nearby where escorting flying boats could land. At Mersah Matruh and Aboukir near Alexandria, there were established RAF bases.

Crete was a more difficult proposition. For a start, it was not British territory and permission would have to be obtained from the Greek authorities for anything that was planned. Then there was the fact that the island was little more than a spine of mountains running east to west. A landing ground had to be found on the northern side of the mountains so that a plane could be refuelled before it attempted the 8,000-feet climb over the mountain range and across the Mediterranean.

At that time Crete still suffered, like the Balkans, from religious conflict. The Turks had captured the island from the Venetians in the seventeenth century and partly occupied it. As usual in such circumstances, militant religious belief led to massacres of Greeks by Turks and Turks by Greeks. It was so bloody that the European Powers established a protectorate there in 1897. The massacres diminished but were not eliminated.

The four power protectorate of Britain, France, Russia and Italy, was called the International Council of Admirals and a naval base was established at Suda Bay, which was the only suitable anchorage on the island.[3] It was not an altruistic project. All four powers saw Crete as strategically important. It was conveniently close to the Suez Canal and it lay at the entrance to the Aegean and the Dardanelles, which were in turn the gateway to the Black Sea and Russia. Before 1914 one third of Britain's grain imports came from Black Sea ports.

The barracks built by the Royal Navy at Suda in 1897 when the International Council of Admirals intervened to stop the fighting between Greeks and Turks. In 1919, when my father took the photo, it was occupied by Bulgarian prisoners of war who hung their laundry out to dry on the bushes in front of the barracks. The POWs later proved useful for hauling aeroplanes out of the mud. (LGS)

Each of the occupying powers at Suda had its own pier with a flagstaff at the end and a house on the shore. The Royal Navy, being the major maritime power, also had a barracks, a clubhouse and a canteen for naval ratings, located inside the former Turkish dockyard or arsenal.

At the end of the Graeco-Turkish war of 1912–13 Crete was finally annexed to Greece, despite British attempts to prevent it because the King of Greece was pro-German. On 1 December 1913 the Greek flag was raised at the Firka Fortress in Chania in the presence of King Constantine, Crown Prince George and Eletherios Venizelos, the Cretan resistance leader. Britain, France, Russia and Italy, much to their regret, evacuated the naval base at Suda in January 1914 and the Greek Navy took it over.

Unlike King Constantine, who was married to a sister of the Kaiser, Venizelos became a supporter of the Allies during the war and later became the first democratically elected prime minister of Greece.

All was changed by the outbreak of the war. The Russians had coveted the sea route to the Mediterranean for centuries and the Turks were naturally anti-Russian. Sentiments had not changed since the Crimean War. The Turks proposed a mutual defence treaty with Germany, which was signed as the war broke out. The two German warships, *Goeben* and *Breslau*, were at large in the Mediterranean and were chased into Constantinople by the Royal Navy. Once safely in harbour, they were nominally transferred to the Turkish Navy but retained their German crews. The Dardanelles was closed to Russian shipping and on 1 November Turkey declared war on the Allies. The Greek Cretans and most other Greeks were now wholly on the Allies' side and the Arab revolt against the Turks began in 1916. There was a substantial minority of Turks (or more accurately Muslims) living on Crete but they, wisely, kept quiet and survived there until 1923, when a compulsory exchange of religiously alien populations took place between Greece and Turkey.

The Royal Navy returned to its original base at Suda as soon as the war broke out and the Royal Naval Air Service established a seaplane base there, which became the southern outpost of the Royal Navy's Aegean Squadron.

The seaplanes used were mostly Short 184s of pre-war design but there were later some Felixstowe F2 and F3 flying boats. These were based on the American Glenn Curtiss flying boats and known as 'Liberty boats' or 'America boats' and, incidentally, the only aeroplanes of American design to have an aggressive role in the war.[4] The American boats were intended for anti-submarine patrols but the demand exceeded the supply and there was rarely more than one at Suda Bay and frequently none at all. The Admiralty gave priority to its bases in Alexandria and Malta.

Having taken the decision to have an airfield for landplanes somewhere on Crete, the Air Ministry now looked to the staff at the seaplane base to find a suitable site and prepare it. It was already 7 July and Brigadier Borton proposed to commence his flight to Egypt just two weeks later.

The hunt for a suitable site did not take long. Crete is mostly rocks and mountains but on the north coast there is a neck of low flat land that links Suda Bay with Chania and separates the mountains of the mainland from the hills of the Akrotiri peninsula. The site that was eventually chosen for the airfield was about one mile west of the western tip of Suda Bay itself and therefore two miles west of the seaplane base. The south of the site was bounded by olive groves and the Chania to Suda Bay road.

The seaplane base inside the old Turkish Arsenal at Suda in 1919. The pier is one of the four that served the ships of the International Council of Admirals. The village of Suda and the officers' mess are behind the trees. The barracks are just off the left of the photo. (LGS)

Immediately south of the road the mountains that form the spine of Crete begin. To the north of the site chosen are the hills running up to the Akrotiri peninsula. It was not an ideal site but it had the advantage that it could be serviced from the existing seaplane base just down the road.[5]

The Navy negotiated with the Greek Governor to lease a strip of land, about 1,000 yards long and 500 yards wide, from local farmers. It was flat but traversed by many drainage ditches because the hills on either side drained the winter rains down to this sheep meadow on their way into Suda Bay. Something had

The seaplane hangar with a tennis court beside it. Launching a seaplane involved up to thirty naval ratings wearing rubber waders up to their armpits in the sea. Once floating, a seaplane could take off in 400 yards. (LGS)

A British-built 'Large America' flying boat. Underneath it is the trolley, on which it was towed sideways into the water by a team of naval ratings. (Q67581)

to be done about this before it was fit for an aeroplane to land. The Navy from the seaplane base got to work.

The labour force consisted of about 100 Greek soldiers whose army pay was small and who were disinclined to work. The British seaplane base had a staff that included ten officers and the naval officer selected to manage the project was Lieutenant

The site selected for the airstrip before work began. The land between the airstrip and Suda Bay was frequently waterlogged but at least it was flat. It is now a housing estate. In the background is the spine of mountains that runs along Crete. (Air 2/80)

41

W.K. Halliday. He overcame the disinclination to work by paying a bonus. Every man was given a chit on which his hours of work were recorded. There was always one naval officer on watch (literally) and any man caught idling had his chit endorsed with a 'fine'. When the airstrip was completed the soldiers presented their chits directly to Lieutenant Halliday and were each paid in cash for the hours for which they had worked less any fines incurred. Payment directly to the individual soldiers was found to be more reliable than payment via their officers or NCOs. Old Mediterranean customs were difficult to eradicate.

The only equipment available for the job was a hutful of shovels without handles, a small steam roller loaned by the public works department, an ancient Ford T truck and a motorcycle. Borton's plane was due to land a fortnight after they started work and two vital days were lost finding handles for the shovels. The fields that had to be levelled were criss-crossed with drainage ditches and there was only time to fill them in and run the steam roller over the top. Since it was midsummer and the dry season when Borton's plane came through en route for Egypt, this seemed adequate. The Navy reported the airfield ready for use.

The monocled Brigadier Borton and Major McLaren, accompanied by two of the best mechanics on the staff at Cranwell, Flight Sergeant Goldfinch and Air Mechanic Francis, left Cranwell in a brand-new Handley Page O/400 C9681 on 25 July 1918. Obtaining a new aircraft was easy. Handley Page bombers were pouring out of several British factories in readiness for the build-up of the Independent Air Force, which was intended to bomb Germany's industrial heartland in 1919. No one knew that the war would be over before that could happen.

The plane was stripped of all non-essentials to reduce weight but it did carry a number of spare parts, which in the event were not needed. Brigadier Borton said afterwards that he would carry the same spares if he made the trip again. Weight was critically important in the matter of range and ceiling height; so critical that Borton declined to carry a wireless even though his destroyer escort over the Mediterranean would have them. It would have weighed at least fifty pounds. He did, however, carry a spare propeller, which was lashed to the top of the fuselage.

Borton and McLaren made a refuelling stop at Manston before setting off for Paris. At Manston they were met by Biffy's parents

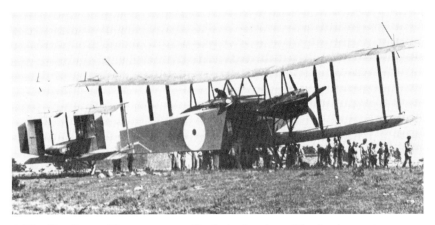

A Handley Page with a spare propeller lashed on top of the fuselage. (Chaz Bowyer)

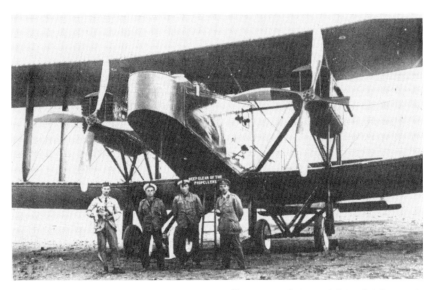

Brigadier Borton and his crew with Handley Page C 9681. Major McLaren is holding his terrier Tiny who flew to Egypt with him three times in Handley Page bombers. (Air 1/913/204/5/854)

and McLaren's wife. Here are three extracts from the diary of retired Lieutenant Colonel A.C. Borton JP who was Biffy's father:

> **July 24th.** Just after breakfast I was on the esplanade and saw a machine DH9 out over the sea about half a mile away. Suddenly the plane came down at a steep gradient and when

about 150 feet from the sea, the left wing broke away. She turned over rapidly several times and fell into the sea. No boat could get to her for a quarter of an hour and although parts of the plane still floated, the bodies of the pilot and observer disappeared and were carried away by the tide. A sad sight indeed.

July 25th. At 9am we first caught sight of the Handley Page in the far distance and she soon came to earth, making a most perfect landing, piloted by Major McLaren. The first to leave the machine was his little dog Tiny. Biffy was looking very fit. We waited to see the H.P. fold up her wings and go into the shed then went back to the hotel. After dinner Biffy, McLaren and I were watching a plane on the sea front when she made a bad turn (too flat) and then a sharp spiral dive into the sea, just clearing the rocks. I got my glasses and could see the pilot sitting on the wreckage, much to my relief, for I thought he must have been killed. He escaped with only a few nasty cuts about his face.

July 28th. At 2.30pm we went to Manston aerodrome, the air full of machines, some looping, and the great H.P. standing outside the shed with her wings spread ready for her voyage. When her two propellers and engines, each 350hp, were in full swing the roar was stupendous. At 3.15 she taxied out on to the ground, turned round, rose very easily into the air, made one small circuit when we waved our farewells and she was soon out of sight.

These diary extracts serve to show just how frequent aeroplane crashes were during the war years. Many more airmen were killed learning to fly than died in action.

Brigadier Borton and his crew crossed the Channel and arrived at Buc, just west of Paris, without incident. The officers booked into a bistro for the night and headed into Paris for dinner at Les Ambassadeurs. Meanwhile, Flight Sergeant Goldfinch and Air Mechanic Francis checked over the machine and refuelled ready for an early start the next day. Flights always began early in the morning before the sun had risen sufficiently to cause air turbulence.

They took off at dawn, sniffed the aroma of the pine trees as they flew over the forest of Fontainebleau, and arrived at Lyon before lunch. That night they slept in a packing case and were off again at first light. They flew down the Rhone valley and landed at Istres, near Marseille, at midday. Now there was work to do. A tail skid had broken, a puncture had to be repaired and they decided to change one propeller. The work took them into the evening to complete and they were devoured by mosquitoes while they did it. On 31 July they took off from Istres and headed along the coast to Nice and Monte Carlo.

The quotations that follow are all taken from Biffy Borton's letters home to his father.

> The view was wonderful. White villas and houses dotted about everywhere and the coastal road and the railway trying to hang on by the eyebrows to the face of the cliff. The prospect of a forced landing, had we been travelling in a single-engined machine would have been uninviting, as in most places there was no beach to speak of, the hills falling almost sheer into the sea. About half an hour before reaching Pisa I handed over again to Mac who made a faultless landing at Pisa.

Borton's comments about the prospects for a single-engined machine if forced to land along this mountainous coast of the Bay of Genoa were prophetic. A later Handley Page was in just this predicament at just this place the following year. It had two engines but they were not enough to save it.

They left Pisa at 6.30 the next morning and Borton took a good photo of the baptistery, the cathedral and the leaning tower. Another easy journey brought them to Centocelle airfield outside Rome and they spent the afternoon sightseeing in Rome. They dined in style in the evening but once again they slept under the aircraft and were savaged by mosquitoes.

Next morning they took off, as usual as dawn was breaking, and headed down the coast towards Naples:

> At 6.15am, after we had been going for about an hour and a half, I handed over to Mac and ten minutes later we reached Naples. I retain a delightful impression of the bay but we couldn't waste time admiring the scenery for in front of us was

Borton's photo of the baptistery, the cathedral and the leaning tower of Pisa, more or less in line, at dawn on 1 August 1918. The airfield is just off the picture to the left. (Air 1/913/204/5/854)

Vesuvius. It was all so very impressive, the town below us, the bay on our right and ahead, slightly to our left, Vesuvius with a column of smoke drifting out of the crater. We passed right over the lip, looking straight down into the hole. After it things generally were an anticlimax and Mac made a faultless landing at Otranto at 9.50 – 370 miles in 5 hours and 10 minutes!

We left Otranto early in the morning, leaving everything behind that we could possibly dispense with in order to have a minimum load for the cross sea trips. The crossing of the Adriatic was simple as soon after leaving the coast we could make out Faro island 50 miles from Otranto and could just see where Corfu lay 20 miles beyond. After leaving Corfu we voyaged down the Greek coast and finally we could distinguish details of the Cretan coast and could make out Chania and the promontory between it and Suda Bay. The aerodrome had been wonderfully well done and was marked with a white chalk boundary and a large landing T to show us exactly where to touch ground.

Borton's photo of Vesuvius, taken on the morning of 2 August 1918. (Air2/83/B4735)

When he landed at Suda Bay, after a bumpy approach because of the heat and the hills close by, Borton was greeted by naval officers from the seaplane base who drove to the landing strip in their Model T Ford and took him and his crew back to their mess in Suda for the night. He photographed the Handley Page on the ground with the mountains to the south as a backdrop. Another photograph, taken by Borton before landing, shows the airfield directly below with its boundary marked by barrow loads of white chalk, put there to help the pilot find it.

> We were most hospitably entertained and they bore us no grudge for all the work which had been thrust on them in getting the aerodrome ready for us. The job they had in organising the local Cretan labour in the face of the most ridiculous and unexpected complications, must have been a most Herculean and heartbreaking task.

With the help of Mr Potamitakis, the security officer at the Suda Bay Greek naval base, I was taken to find the airstrip in the summer of 2000. Looking south there is now a builder's yard and

Borton's Handley Page making its east to west approach to the airstrip between Suda and Chania. The photo was taken from the seaplane base in the bay. This was the first landplane ever to touch down on Crete. (Air 2/83/B4735)

looking north a suburb of white, flat-roofed, ferroconcrete houses between some of which run deep concrete lined drainage culverts. No planes will ever land there again. The new airport is five miles away to the east on top of the Akrotiri peninsula.

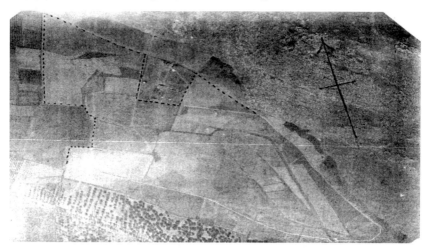

The Suda airstrip as it appeared to Borton. The boundary in the north-west is marked by a dotted line added to the photo later. In the south-east it is marked by barrow loads of white chalk. To the north are the Akrotiri hills. To the south are the olive grove and the road from Chania to Suda. The drainage ditches had been filled in but they are still clearly visible. (Air 2/83/B4735)

48

Brigadier Borton's Handley Page on the ground at Suda with the Ford T from the nearby seaplane base and two white uniformed naval officers in attendance. The airstrip can be precisely located because, in the photograph, the upper port wing of the aeroplane is touching a hamlet on the south side of the Heraklion to Chania road, which is still there today. (Air 1/913/204/5/854)

The aeroplane and its crew had to wait at Suda Bay for three days while the destroyer escort for the Mediterranean crossing got into position. They set off at first light on 7 August. It had been blowing hard from the north during the night, which helped progress as they made their way, first of all east towards Heraklion and then south, well clear of the tallest part of the mountain range. They flew the 395 miles to landfall at Sollum and then east to Mersah Matruh without incident and in fine weather. Two destroyers, HMS *Ribble* and HMS *Colne*, in wireless contact with one another but not with the plane, were stationed, as arranged, along the 395-mile route. Because of crosswinds, the course that the Handley Page took was 30 miles east of the destroyers. There was a haze and neither saw the other. Without radio contact the escort was pointless. After refuelling at Mersah Matruh, the plane arrived safely at Aboukir (Alexandria) that evening.

There they were met by the AOC Middle East – Geoffrey Salmond who was now a major general. He flew with them the next day to the pyramids where they circled for a few minutes while another aeroplane took photographs of them. Then they landed at Heliopolis, eleven days after leaving Manston in Kent. From England it had been a journey of 2,592 miles and taken

The airfield at Sollum on the shore of the Mediterranean. It is all sand but hard enough to land on and used by RAF fighters as a refuelling point. (Air 1/913/204/5/854)

Borton's plane taking off from Aboukir for the last leg of the flight to Cairo. Now he had Major General Geoffrey Salmond with him as a passenger. (Air 1/913/204/5/854)

36 hours and 13 minutes of flying time, at an average speed of 71 mph. The Brigadier was carrying a letter from his father to his cousin, the Postmaster General of Egypt. It was the first airmail letter from England to Egypt and it is now in the Cairo Museum.

An 'enormous concourse' was assembled to greet them and that evening there was a great celebration banquet at which Brigadier Borton made a speech. Many of those present were Australian members of Borton's No. 5 Wing and Ross Smith was among them. He was a distinguished fighter ace and Biffy had got to know him well in the year that Smith had been in No. 1 Squadron.

On 12 August the *Evening Standard* carried these headlines:

TO EGYPT BY AIR

REMARKABLE FEAT BY RAF

FOUR IN ONE MACHINE

SERVICE MACHINE USED

Brigadier Borton and Major McLaren just after landing at Heliopolis. Borton has a cigarette in his mouth. McLaren is wearing a forage cap and is mostly hidden by an officer with his back to the camera. Major General Salmond is the tall man beside Borton. (Air 1/913/204/5/854)

The fact that one of the headlines is 'Four in one machine' shows just how unusual the huge Handley Page was so far as the general public was concerned.

This flight was a great achievement. No aeroplane had flown so far and so quickly anywhere in the world before. But the flight

The RAF airfield at Heliopolis in the summer of 1918. Borton's machine, the only Handley Page O/400 then in Egypt, is at the top of the picture. Heliopolis is now a prosperous middle class suburb of Cairo. (Q103609)

was so uneventful that it gave no indication of what was to befall some of those who flew the same route later. In his written report on the flight Brigadier Borton stated:

> A ferry service of machines to the Middle East following the same or a similar course, should prove a perfectly safe and feasible undertaking which would have far reaching results of the very greatest importance.[6]

The success of the flight greatly impressed Major General Geoffrey Salmond who had flown the last leg of the journey from Alexandria to Cairo. In a letter to the Chief of the Air Staff, Major General Sykes, written on 28 August 1918 shortly after Borton's flight had been completed, Major General Salmond set out his proposal:

> I forward herewith the scheme in detail worked out by Major A.S.C. McLaren with a view to establishing an aerial route between England, Italy and the Middle East. The total personnel required for this aerial line of communication is 182 which includes 36 ferry pilots.
>
> This route would be capable of supplying the RAF in Italy, Otranto, Salonika and the Aegean and Egypt.
>
> As regards machines, I see no reason why Bristol fighters, DH9s, Handley Pages, SE 5s and RE 8s should not be sent out by this route.
>
> The saving in shipping and railway traffic would be very large indeed and this is particularly the case as regards Egypt where the demand for service types of machines both for training and for operations will require fully 45 of these service machines per month. At the same time acceptance work would be greatly reduced at all the stations since erection work for all these types would no longer be necessary and this would result in a corresponding decrease in establishments.
>
> I do not consider that winter weather conditions should be allowed to weigh against this scheme since the essence of the scheme is progress and climatic difficulties can undoubtedly be overcome.
>
> I recommend that this scheme should receive very close attention for I am strongly of the opinion that the sooner it is established the greater will be the efficiency of the RAF as whole.

I also recommend that Major A.S.C. McLaren should be at once detailed to organise this line of communication since he has had experience of the Route himself and has also the necessary initiative to work it out in detail.

W.G H. Salmond Major General
Commanding RAF Middle East. 26.8.18

Major McLaren's detailed report on the flight is also in the file and it is worth highlighting one remark from it:

The enormous saving in time will at once be apparent as also will be the saving in losses due to enemy action with submarines.

Another supporter of the scheme was Brigadier P.R.C. Groves, the Director of Flying Operations at the Air Ministry. With Major General Sykes, he was an advocate of the policy to maintain an Air Force of sixty-two squadrons after the war with another ninety-two in skeleton form and thus maintain Britain's position as the leading air power in the world. For this, long-distance aerial routes with servicing and refuelling airfields every 400 miles would be required. One such route would be from England to Egypt via Italy and Greece.

To Geoffrey Salmond's proposal the Chief of the Air Staff replied on 3 October:

I agree generally, though present operations in the Near and Middle East may necessitate some modifications.

But not everybody was as enthusiastic. The Comptroller of Equipment RAF, Major General E.H. Ellington, had much practical experience of sending replacement machines from England to British squadrons on the Western Front. In a letter to the Chief of the Air Staff on 5 October he said:

1. As a practical means of delivering machines to Salonika and the Middle East I do not think this scheme has anything to commend it. Even over the short distance of the Channel we are frequently prevented by weather from delivering any

machines for several days at a time and the experience we have had in delivering machines by air to the Independent Air Force shows that an average of about 5 days is taken on the journey from the time the machine leaves the Acceptance Park until it arrives at the Independent Air Force depot.

2. The estimate given on page 3 of Major McLaren's detailed report, that the machines will only take 6 days from England to Egypt is absurd. The only experience we have had so far is General Borton's Handley Page, which after several false starts took 10 days in the finest time of the year and the second HP, which although it started a considerable time ago, has not yet arrived.

3. The estimate of personnel required is I think very much below what will be found necessary if the scheme is adopted.

Ellington gives several reasons for this, which appear to be sound but need not concern us. He also draws attention to the large number of spares for every type of machine that will have to be stored all along the route.

> The above are my reasons for not adopting this proposal as a practical means of delivering machines to the Middle East. If however from the point of view of policy, it is considered desirable to establish a route by air to Egypt, I think we should confine it to one type, say DH9, which, as far as I can see, will be forthcoming in sufficient numbers to justify this method of delivery which I am satisfied would prove very costly.[7]

A week later Ellington followed this up with another letter to the Chief of the Air Staff:

> The attached may interest you in connection with the proposal to despatch machines by air to Egypt and Salonika. It shows that in a period of three weeks in September, 5 machines out of 29 DH9s crashed en route to Courban and that the average time taken was 4.25 days. Although September was not a fine month it was probably no worse than the average of 12 months from the point of view of delivering machines.
> Salonika is four times as far as Courban.[8] If we take this experience as a guide, we should expect to lose 64% of machines

during delivery to Salonika and 96% during delivery to Egypt. The time taken would be respectively 17 and 25 days. We may hope that the percentage of crashes in this case is abnormal but it shows that delivery by air over long distances is not so rapid or so economical a method as is sometimes considered.[9]

Salonika is mentioned, as well as the Middle East, because the war was still in progress and the Allies had half a million troops and two RAF squadrons there.

But the Director of Flying Operations, Brigadier P.R.C. Groves, continued to support Salmond. In his letter to the Chief of the Air Staff, Groves replied to Ellington's misgivings as follows:

> The figures shown in Ellington's minute preceding are certainly striking but I do not consider that they should be accepted in themselves without further investigation, as a condemnation of the proposed scheme for the formation of 'Ferry Pilots Middle East'.
>
> As regards the comparative losses to be expected from the alternative means of transit, I think the contention that the air route is likely to involve the loss of more machines than transport by sea, with submarines and other dangers, is open to question. A ship sunk means the complete loss of the machines on board. On the other hand, though a proportion of forced landings is to be expected when proceeding by air, with good pilots, crashes entailing a 'write-off' without even partial salvage are likely to be a very rare occurrence. In the last nine months 20 machines have actually been lost during transit by sea to the Middle East whilst a further 26 were torpedoed but salvaged.
>
> In my opinion, the scheme, if found practicable, should be put into effect as early as possible in view of the increasing range of machines and the desirability, on the grounds of policy, of inaugurating this route as a step towards the development of aerial transport after the war.[10]

These opinions were all given while the war was still in progress and there was no thought of it ending only five weeks later.

*   *   *

After the first Handley Page arrived in Egypt Major McLaren returned to England to ferry out two more Handley Page bombers. The first (C9700) had an uneventful journey and landed at Heliopolis on 5 October.

McLaren then returned to England again and made a third flight, this time in a Handley Page V/1500. This was a similar design to the O/400 but more powerful because it had four engines mounted in two pairs back to back. It weighed 7 tons empty compared with the 3½ tons of its twin-engined predecessor and had almost double the wing area. Some 3 tons of its all-up weight was accounted for by the 1,000 gallons of fuel that it carried. Its very bulk proved its undoing later when competing with the newly commissioned Vickers Vimy. The Vimy had the same engines as the twin-engined Handley Page but was much smaller and weighed only 3 tons empty. It could carry 50 per cent more petrol than the O/400 so that its range was significantly greater.

The HP V/1500 was brought into service in the last week of the war and would have bombed Berlin if the Armistice had not intervened. Only about forty were ever built and of these one went to Newfoundland for an unsuccessful attempt on the Transatlantic Prize. It had repeated mechanical problems and, by the time these were sorted out, Alcock and Brown had won the prize in a Vimy. Another V/1500 crash-landed on a beach on the return journey from a pioneering flight to Madrid and was lost in the rising tide.

McLaren took off in the huge four-engined machine for his third flight to Egypt on 25 November. Although this machine eventually flew as far as Delhi, it would be misleading to describe the flight as successful. There were many delays because of bad weather but the outstanding feature of the flight was the large number of mechanical breakdowns en route. To list them would require a chapter in itself. As with Borton in the first flight, a flying boat escort was arranged using a boat from Alexandria but it was wrecked somewhere along the Greek coast and the crew and the wreckage were brought into Suda Bay by a trawler.

Before McLaren reached Crete in this machine, Suda had already telegraphed to say that the airfield was flooded and unusable so McLaren changed his route and flew south from Taranto to the Straits of Messina and Sicily, heading for Malta. It was so bumpy that for ten minutes both pilots were hanging on to the controls together and dripping with sweat. The turbulence that they experienced may have been unexpected by them but it was well known to others. Rear Admiral Mark Kerr had commanded the British Adriatic Squadron of the Royal Naval Air Service in 1917 and this is what he had to say about air turbulence around Greece and Italy:

> Alternate mountains and plains in a hot climate, produce alternate layers of hot and cold air, resulting in really wonderful bumps such as I have not seen equalled elsewhere. I have seen the height meter register a rise of 200 feet in two seconds which means that there was a rising current travelling at about 70mph. Mountain peaks can produce vortices sufficiently strong to turn a machine over.[11]

They flew along the Sicilian coast at 100 feet to avoid the clouds with crowds watching from below who had probably never seen an aeroplane before. When they landed at Catania their wheels sank deep into mud and it took seventy Italian soldiers to pull them out. Two days later they got away again and had an easy two-hour flight to Valetta where they landed on the polo ground. They had calm weather to Benghazi and then 500 miles over the desert to Mersah Matruh without seeing a single living thing, animal or plant.

On this leg of the journey the gearing of the front starboard engine crumbled and they were reduced to three engines. An hour later the same thing happened to the rear starboard engine and they could not continue on two port engines only. They made a forced landing a mile away from the coastal road and attracted the attention of some passing Bedouin to whom they gave three sovereigns to take a message the fifty miles into Mersah Matruh with the promise of more if they were rescued. Then they sat down and had a meal of corned beef and champagne while they waited ... and waited. At night they made a flare from a petrol can and lighted it as darkness fell. Every hour they fired a Verey's light. The next day cars came along the road and they were picked up and taken into Mersah Matruh. As they were lunching with the Governor of the Western Desert, the Bedouin arrived and claimed their just reward of another two sovereigns.

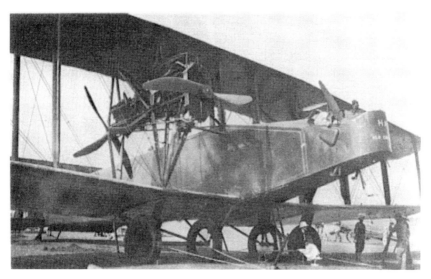

McLaren's Handley Page V/1500 after it had arrived in India. McLaren and McEwen were old boys of Charterhouse School and the machine has the name *Old Carthusian* painted round its nose. The tractor engines have only twin-bladed propellers. The pusher engines have four-bladed propellers. (Air 2/83/B4735)

The machine was given an overhaul at Heliopolis, but even so had two more forced landings on the way to Karachi, which it reached thirty-three days after it had set out from England. When it came down for the second time, the engines were in such a bad

McLaren's view of Mount Etna as they flew over Sicily. (Air1/2689/15/312/126)

state that the machine could not take off again with the load it was carrying. The VIP on board, Brigadier McEwen was disembarked because he had sunstroke and one fitter was also discarded. They continued to Karachi by ship. The machine did not reach Delhi, its intended destination, until 23 February. It was in such poor condition that it was laid up. The bad experience with this four-engined Handley Page, and with the one that pioneered the route to Madrid and ended up in the sea off Biarritz, may well have contributed to a preference for the more modern Vickers Vimy, which later became the first choice for long-distance attempts. The Vimy was a better aircraft but the first one did not commence flying trials until November 1917 and so no Vimys took part in the war.

Major McLaren wrote a detailed account of the flight in the four-engined Handley Page[12] but, apart from some whimsy about his pet dog Tiny and a catalogue of the mechanical breakdowns, the one piece of prose that stands out is this account of an incident between Baghdad and Karachi:

> Soon after leaving Bandar Rig we had a little amusement at the expense of one of the natives of the country. We were flying at about 100 feet when we saw, a short distance ahead, an unlucky native who was attempting to bathe by the banks of a small stream and was consequentially not in a position to argue his point with us. We put the nose of the machine down and headed straight for this unhappy mortal, who, already petrified with fear, at once threw up his arms to Allah and called loudly for help. At a distance of 50 yards I fired a green Verey's light at him which burst into flames in front of his feet. His morale became entirely disorganised and he fell flat on his face into the stream. On looking back however, we saw him struggling out and I have no doubt that he thought the end of the world had come.[13]

The contrast between McLaren and Lawrence in their attitude to the Arabs could not be more acute. McLaren's 'prank' highlights the dismissive attitude of Westerners, which led to Britain and France, and later the USA, regarding the political aspirations of Arabs as unimportant. The foundations for 9/11 and 7/7 were laid a long time ago.

The nose of a Handley Page made of plywood bent round a wooden frame. Brigadier McEwen was sitting right in the nose. Hence his 'grandstand view'. (Q12181)

Apart from trail blazing, the purpose of McLaren's flight was to deliver the newly appointed Air Officer Commanding India to his job. What Brigadier N.D.K. McEwen CMG DSO had to say about terrorizing this local inhabitant is not recorded. McEwen was travelling in the forward gunner's cockpit so, as well as getting sunstroke, he had a grandstand view of this unprovoked attack on this 'unhappy mortal'.

Perhaps it acclimatized him to the way in which the British Raj subdued its subjects. Four months after Brigadier McEwen arrived in India, his mess colleague, Brigadier Dyer, massacred 379 unarmed demonstrators in an enclosed square at Amritsar on 11 April 1919. Dyer was exonerated at the subsequent enquiry but sacked when the first Labour Government under Ramsay MacDonald was elected four years later.

Notes

1. The only evidence for the success of this attack was the report of the crew of the Handley Page. After the raid the Turkish Minister at Berne said that a torpedo boat had been hit but not the *Goeben* and

that the only damage at the Turkish War Office was to a stable block. But the medals had been awarded by then and the story was good propaganda. Air 2/79/B2115.

2. Air 1/649/17/122/402.
3. ADM/1/8396/354.
4. Because it lacked the impetus of war, the USA in 1917 was way behind Europe in the development of aviation despite the start given by the Wright brothers.
5. Air 1/913/204/5/854, Air 2/82/B4662, Air 2/79/B8044.
6. Air 1/913/204/5/854.
7. Air 2/82/B4662.
8. In Burgundy SE of Troyes.
9. Air 2/82/B4662.
10. Air 2/82/B4662.
11. *Land, Sea and Air – Reminiscences of Admiral Sir Mark Kerr*. Longmans, 1927. Kerr was the pilot of the V/1500 that failed to make the trans-atlantic crossing from Newfoundland.
12. Air 1/462/15/312/126, Air 1/2386/228/11/8.
13. Air 1/2689/15/312/126.

CHAPTER 5

The End of the War with Turkey

While Borton was away in England collecting the Handley Page, No. 1 Squadron of the Australian Flying Corps further distinguished itself. During the two months preceding General Allenby's September 1918 offensive, this squadron alone shot down fifteen enemy aircraft and drove down twenty-seven more. Many of the machines that were driven down were then shot up on the ground and had to be written off. Their pilots suffered the same fate. Papers later recovered from the captured Turkish headquarters at Nazareth confirmed these figures.

The air supremacy achieved in the run-up to Allenby's final offensive was complete. In one week in June hostile aeroplanes crossed into British-held territory 100 times but they came over at 18,000 feet, which made accurate observation impossible. In the last week of August the number of enemy sorties dropped to eighteen and in the two following weeks immediately before the offensive only four enemy aircraft appeared. None at all were seen in the week before the Allenby offensive began.

In July Major General Geoffrey Salmond visited No. 1 Squadron at its base at Ramleh between Jaffa and Jerusalem and then declared:

> No. 1 Squadron is one of the best squadrons in the Royal Air Force. Its interior economy, workshops and discipline are excellent. The turn-out of its mechanical transport, and

above all of its aeroplanes, are models of their kind. On this squadron has always fallen a large portion of the work which has had to be performed by the Royal Air Force in Palestine since the day that the Egyptian Expeditionary Force left the Canal. It is a matter of pride to me to have had this squadron under my command since the days of its formation.[1]

The first Handley Page that had arrived in Egypt (C9681) was overhauled at Heliopolis and then on 29 August it was flown by Brigadier Borton to the No. 1 Squadron base at Ramleh. As might be expected, the Handley Page was allotted to Ross Smith who was now a captain. Major McLaren had returned to England to bring out another machine, so Brigadier Borton showed Ross Smith how to fly it.

General Allenby and Lawrence were now working in concert. On the eve of Allenby's offensive in the Nablus hills on 19 September 1918, Allenby asked Lawrence to mount a diversionary attack on the Turks at Dera'a, an important rail junction that was well inland from Megiddo, Allenby's intended objective.[2] Lawrence and the Arabs complied and both Dera'a station and the railway lines north, south and west of it were destroyed. All means of supply from the north to the Turkish 7th and 8th Armies, which were facing Allenby, were cut off and the Turkish 4th Army,

The Handley Page that Borton flew to Egypt taking part in Allenby and Lawrence's campaign to drive the Turks out of Palestine, Syria and Transjordan. The cockpit is shrouded to keep out the heat and the propeller blades are canvas covered to try to prevent them warping or cracking. (Chaz Bowyer)

based in Jordan was unable to come to the aid of the 7th and 8th. The Turks assumed that this was the major offensive and began to move troops inland to meet it. Without aerial reconnaissance General Liman von Sanders had no idea that General Allenby was massing British, Australian and Indian troops for an attack on Megiddo, close to the Palestinian coast.

At the very moment that Allenby's attack on Megiddo was launched, Ross Smith flew the Handley Page to attack the Turkish Headquarters and the telephone exchange at El Afule. He dropped sixteen 112-pound bombs and wrecked the telephone exchange and the nearby railway junction. This cut all communications between the Turkish Headquarters and the Turkish 7th and 8th Armies. It also resulted in two divisions of the Turkish Army being trapped in the narrow Wadi al Fara'a the next day where other RAF planes destroyed them.[3]

Borton later wrote home this account of what had happened:

> The most remarkable feature of the operations is what can be achieved by organised bombing. On at least four occasions we have completely blocked the retreating columns, but one occasion stands out in which we caught a column retreating through a narrow gorge in the hills. We bombed it incessantly for four hours, completely blocking the head of the column and creating the most appalling carnage. A length of road some five miles long, was absolutely packed and you can get some idea of what it meant from the subsequent count – Over 80 guns and 700 horses and motor transport were found in an inextricable mess on just this one stretch of road. General Salmond who came up to stay with me, went out to the scene next day and was absolutely appalled at the havoc which could be produced by aircraft. We are commonly alluded to as the butchers now.

Clive Conrick, the observer in one of the No. 1 Squadron AFC machines, was an eye witness of the action. This is what he wrote afterwards:

> Chips of rock fly off the rock face and red splotches suddenly appear on the Turks who would stop climbing and fall and their bodies were strewn along the base of the cliff like a lot of

The scene after the two retreating Turkish divisions had been caught by the RAF in the Wadi al Fara'a on 21 September. Without previous experience of air attack, they had been crowded together in broad daylight and were unable to spread out laterally because of the steep hillsides. The men scrambled up the hillsides and dispersed but the horses and the transport were all destroyed. (IWM Q12310)

> dirty rags. When we were climbing again to renew the attack I had a better opportunity to machine gun the troops and the transports on the road.

General Salmond wrote his account of the Wadi al Fara'a attack and sent it to his wife in England:

> No picture of retreat that you have ever seen, can equal this column, over six miles long, packed with dead horses, dead mules, dead oxen, dead Turks, motor lorries overturned, lorries that had eventually caught fire, guns, over 80 of them – all abandoned. All control of personnel went by the board, and the result was almost complete demoralisation. This is the true secret of the extraordinarily rapid victory.[4]

This battle was the turning point in the war with Turkey. The Turkish troops were demoralized and put up no further serious resistance.

Immediately following this victory, Lawrence flew in a Be2c to Allenby's headquarters and made an urgent request for Bristol fighters to assist him against enemy aircraft which on his own eastern front were still troublesome. Lawrence had two Be2cs attached to his desert army but they were no match for the Fokkers that were harassing the Arab forces. The success of the Arab diversionary attacks around Dera'a had greatly enhanced Lawrence's standing with General Allenby who now realized just how important Feisal, Lawrence and the Arabs had become. Allenby detached two Bristol fighters and a DH9A from No. 1 Squadron and sent them to assist Feisal and Lawrence with reconnaissance for their own inland advance towards Syria. Needless to say, Ross Smith was one of the Bristol fighter pilots selected for this task. They were to be based at Um el Surab, about 100 miles east of No. 1 Squadron's base and so aviation fuel, ammunition and spare parts for the Bristols and the DH9A had to be supplied as well as the machines themselves. This was a task for the Handley Page.

On 22 September Ross Smith flew over to Um el Surab to size up a landing ground for the Handley Page. While he was there an incident occurred that Lawrence included in *The Seven Pillars Of Wisdom*.

> Meanwhile it was breakfast time with a smell of sausage in the air. We sat round, very ready: but the watcher on the tower yelled 'Aeroplane up!', seeing one coming over from Dera'a. Our Australians scrambled wildly to their yet-hot machines and started them in a moment. Ross Smith with his observer leaped into one and climbed like a cat up the sky. Peters followed after him ... There were one enemy two-seater and three scouts. Ross Smith fastened on the big one and after five minutes of sharp machine gun rattle, the German dived suddenly towards the railway line. As it flashed behind the low ridge there broke out a pennon of smoke and from its falling place a soft, dark cloud. An 'Ah' came from the Arabs about us. Five minutes later Ross Smith was back and jumped gaily out of his machine, swearing that the Arab front was the place.[5]

Smith then flew back to Ramleh to pick up the heavily loaded Handley Page. When it arrived the huge size of the machine had an effect on Arab morale as another extract from Lawrence's famous book shows:

> Twenty miles short of Um el Surab we perceived a single Bedawi, running southward all in a flutter, his grey hair and grey beard flying in the wind, and his shirt (tucked up in his belly cord) puffing out behind him. He altered course to pass near us, and, raising his bony arms, yelled 'The biggest aeroplane in the world', before he flapped on into the south, to spread his great news among the tents. (See colour painting.)
>
> At Um el Surab the Handley stood majestic on the grass with Bristols and a 9A like fledglings beneath its spread of wings. Round it admired the Arabs, saying, 'Indeed at last they have sent us THE aeroplane, of which these things were foals'. Before night, rumour of Feisal's resource went over Jebel Ruse and the hollow of Hauran, telling people that the balance was weighted on our side.
>
> Borton himself had come over to concert help. We talked with him while our men drew from her bomb racks and fuselage a ton of petrol; oil and spare parts for Bristol fighters; tea and sugar rations for our men; letters, Reuter telegrams and medicines for us. Then the great machine rose into the early dusk for Ramleh with an agreed programme of night bombing against Dera'a and Mafrak, to complete that ruin of the railway traffic which our gun cotton had begun.[6]

Arab wonder at the sight of a Handley Page. Some of them appear equally fascinated by the camera. (T.E. Lawrence)

Thanks to the rout of the Turkish army both Allenby's and Feisal's forces advanced. The Arabs reached Damascus on 1 October, just a few hours before the British and French troops under Allenby, who were coming by the coastal route.[7] After much argument amongst rival Arab factions, a provisional Arab government under Prince Feisal was immediately proclaimed.

But as soon as General Allenby arrived on 3 October he informed Prince Feisal that his newly appointed Arab government would not be recognized because France and not Hussein was going to take control of Syria. McMahon's promise to Hussein

An elated Prince Feisal. (Q10561)

Lawrence entering Damascus on 1 October 1918. (Rolls-Royce Heritage Trust)

Arab troops on camels entering Damascus as Turkish prisoners are being escorted out. (Q 12367)

General Allenby arriving in Damascus on 3 October 1918. (Q12390)

General Allenby and Prince Feisal.

Prince Feisal entering Damascus on 1 October 1918. (T.E. Lawrence)

of Arab independence was deliberately ambiguous but he had explicitly named Damascus, Homs, Hama and Aleppo and the area east of those towns as coming under Arab control when the war ended, provided that the Arabs had fought to drive out the Turks. They had done this but now Allenby, under instructions from London, which in turn was under pressure from France, reneged on that promise and began to implement the Sykes-Picot Agreement.

On hearing what Allenby had told Feisal, Lawrence was disgusted and requested immediate leave. Allenby, with evident Arab sympathies, readily granted it. Lawrence returned to England to try and rally support for the Arab cause.[8] Prince Feisal likewise hoped to achieve his father's objective with Lawrence's help, by appealing to the delegates at the Paris Peace Conference, and in particular to President Wilson who had firmly advocated self determination for all after the war.

The next day both forces advanced into the Lebanon and a week later took Beirut. The Lebanon was an area that the French

Feisal leaving the *Hotel Victoria* in Damascus on 3 October 1918 after being told by Allenby that the French and not Feisal were going to take control in Syria. (Q12364)

intended to control when the war was over and indeed McMahon had specifically said so in his earlier correspondence with Hussein. But Feisal's troops could not be expected to know the details of the McMahon-Hussein correspondence. They had captured a significant Arab town from the Turks and the Arab flag was hoisted

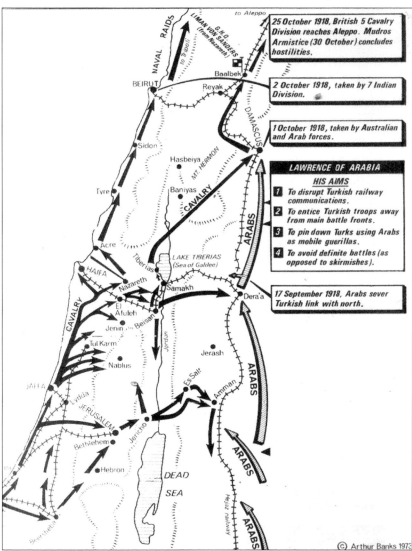

The later stages of the campaign. The Arabs advanced inland while General Allenby and the Egyptian Expeditionary Force advanced along the coast. (Banks, op.cit.)

over it in the name of Prince Feisal. The French objected when they arrived and Allenby ordered the flag to be taken down. The Arabs were furious and riots erupted in Damascus as well as in Beirut. Feisal's army was on the point of mutiny. Feisal appealed for British and French support. The Arabs had played their part in driving out the Turks and now they expected the reward that Sir Henry McMahon had promised them. Allenby could promise them nothing.

It is evident that General Allenby was unhappy at having to treat Prince Feisal in this way but he was under orders from the Cabinet in London. The Arabs were furious and declarations from the British and French governments that Arab interests would be looked after did nothing to mollify them.

In the last month of the war the Turkish retreat continued rapidly and Tripoli, Homs, Hama and Aleppo were taken in three weeks. The collapse of the Turkish armies led to the collapse of the Turkish Government. Armistice negotiations commenced on the Greek island of Lemnos and were concluded on HMS *Agamemnon* in the harbour of Mudros on 30 October 1918. Twelve days later the armistice that ended the Great War was signed in the Forest of Compiègne.

In the Middle East, Britain and France were no longer trusted and for the next six months the Arabs looked to the United States for support.

The following is a resolution passed at the Pan Arab Congress in Damascus in June 1919:

> Desiring that our country should not fall a prey to colonization and believing that the American Nation is farthest from any thought of colonization and has no political ambition in our country, we will seek the technical and economic assistance from the United States of America, provided that such assistance does not exceed twenty years. In the event of America not finding herself in a position to accept our desire for assistance we will seek this assistance from Great Britain. The noble principles enunciated by President Wilson strengthen our confidence that our desires emanating from the depths of our hearts, shall be the decisive factor in determining our future; and that President Wilson and the free American people will be supporters for the realization of our hopes, thereby proving

their sincerity and noble sympathy with the aspiration of the weaker nations in general and our Arab people in particular.[9]

But all this Arab goodwill was squandered. President Wilson had a severe stroke in September 1919 and went into seclusion. The USA became Republican, reverted to isolationism and refused to join the League of Nations, which had been President Wilson's brainchild. Zionism in the USA steadily grew, supported by right wing Christians and came to dominate both Houses of Congress. The seed was sown for the conflict that has continued ever since.

Notes

1. F.M. Cutlack. op. cit.
2. To bible readers Megiddo is better known as Armageddon.
3. Air 1/2393/244/3.
4. Anne Baker, *From Biplane to Spitfire*, Leo Cooper, 2003.
5. T.E. Lawrence , *The Seven Pillars Of Wisdom*, 1939 edition, Reprint Society. p. 639.
6. Ibid p.640.
7. There is evidence that General Allenby deliberately held back his forces so that the Arabs could have the honour of entering Damascus first. Its capture had been the object of their whole campaign. The Australian Light Horse claim that they entered Damascus first. Whether correct or not, this does not affect the promise given to Sherif Hussein by McMahon that this was to be Arab territory when the war was won.
8. Lawrence apparently already knew of the Sykes-Picot agreement in early 1918. Although he disagreed with it, he kept quiet until the war was won. If he knew of the agreement he may well have been hoping to circumvent it by getting Prince Feisal into Damascus first. Ever after his conscience was troubled by his divided loyalties and by the lack of support for the Arab point of view at the Paris Peace Conference.
9. George Antonius, *The Arab Awakening*. Hamish Hamilton 1938.

CHAPTER 6

To India and Beyond

For a brief interlude after the armistice General Salmond was free to indulge his new-found enthusiasm for the Handley Page. The second machine (C9700), which Major McLaren had ferried to Egypt, arrived at Heliopolis on 5 October 1918 and when the armistice came it was lying idle at Aboukir.

Generals Salmond and Borton had flown together in C9681 from Aboukir to Heliopolis when it first reached Egypt and with Ross Smith as pilot it had been active in support of Allenby's campaign. Now it needed another overhaul. They decided to try to fly C9700 to Baghdad, a journey across 900 miles of desert, without maps and with only the tracks of camel caravans to guide them. If all went well they planned to continue the journey all the way to India, which was the furthest point of General Salmond's Middle Eastern Command.

Salmond was not an experienced pilot and so Borton again chose Ross Smith as second pilot. By this time Smith was probably more experienced in flying a Handley Page than Borton. The mechanics were two more Australians, Sergeant Bennett and Sergeant Shiers, personally chosen by Ross Smith and probably the most able mechanics in No. 1 Squadron. The machine was moved to Heliopolis for overhaul and on 29 November they took off for Baghdad, carrying a ten-day supply of food and water in case they had a forced landing in the desert. The route that they chose carefully skirted the vast area of waterless desert that lies on the direct line between Cairo and the Persian Gulf. See colour map.

C9700, the Handley Page that McLaren had brought out from England and which Borton and Ross Smith flew from Cairo to Baghdad and India with Major General Geoffrey Salmond as passenger, photographed just before take-off from Cairo. (Borton)

On the first day they flew over the Nile Delta, across the Suez Canal, over Jerusalem and on to Damascus where they spent the night. The next day they flew on over featureless black lava and then over the desert until they crossed the Euphrates. They touched down at Baghdad a little over seven hours after leaving Damascus. The whole journey from Cairo had taken two days, of which 12½ hours were in the air. The weather had been perfect all the way. The desert could not be crossed by car and by camel it would have taken between two and three weeks.

Elated by their success they flew on to Bushire on the Persian Gulf, Karachi, Delhi and finally Calcutta, which they reached on 12 December 1918. The Viceroy, Frederick Napier, later Lord Chelmsford, greeted them as they landed and there were great celebrations.

The Times reported:

> The flight was not taken in an attempt to fly against time, but to place General Salmond in a position to advise the Government of India on the best route to be followed in future.

The atmosphere conditions are favourable for an un-interrupted service to be maintained all the year round over the route and it is understood that there are no difficulties in the way of a regular service which cannot be overcome.

When the news reached England, Lieutenant Colonel Arthur C. Borton JP, Brigadier Borton's father, at the family seat at Cheveney, near Yalding in Kent, opened a bottle of 1882 port to celebrate and carefully recorded the news in the fifth volume of his diary of the war. He also wrote:

I was reading my father's Afghan War Diary of 1840 today and it took him four months and eleven days to sail from Kent to Calcutta. His grandson Biffy did it in 72 hours 13 minutes actual flying or three days and nights and thirteen minutes.

Biffy Borton's father, Lieutenant Colonel A.C. Borton JP, the squire of his village and a pillar of the Edwardian establishment. (Slater)

Tempora mutantur. I wonder how long it will take Biffy's grandson, say in 1998. My forecast is three hundred miles an hour. – Say sixteen hours.[1]

The ambitions of Borton and Ross Smith grew. If they could reach Calcutta what was to stop them from carrying on to Australia? So they planned a survey by ship to select suitable landing strips and to lay down stocks of petrol at each one. Then they intended to return to India, pick up the Handley Page and fly on to Australia in the summer of 1919.

With the permission of the Air Ministry they set off on their survey in the Royal Indian Mail Ship *Sphinx*, with 7,000 gallons of petrol on 10 February 1919. Only two days out from Calcutta the

9700 after the dust storm. (Both photos via Chaz Bowyer)

ship caught fire and was completely destroyed. Brigadier Borton and Ross Smith narrowly escaped with their lives.

The Indian Government, which was of course British, provided a second ship RIMS *Minto*, but only on condition that the ship carried no cargo of petrol. This meant that they could undertake the survey but not distribute the stocks of aviation fuel along the route. So for the next three months they surveyed the route over Burma, Siam (Thailand), Malaya, Singapore, the Dutch East Indies (Indonesia) and finally East Timor, which was only 350 miles from Darwin in the Northern Territory of Australia. They then returned to India only to find that their Handley Page had been commandeered by the military authorities and used in a campaign on the North West Frontier. It was standing at Risalpur and about to make a bombing raid on Kabul when a violent dust storm arose. Despite being securely pegged down and surrounded by lorries to protect it, it was smashed over on to its back and had to be written off.[2] C9681 fared better and was known still to be in service with No. 216 Squadron at Khartoum in 1920.

Notes

1. Guy Slater (Ed.), *My Warrior Sons, The Borton Family Diary 1914–1918*, Peter Davies, 1973
2. Chaz Bowyer, *Handley Page Bombers of World War 1* and Ross Smith in the *National Geographic Magazine*.

CHAPTER 7

The Arab World Erupts

After the arrival of C9700 in Calcutta on 12 December and the celebrations that followed, Major General Salmond managed three weeks' leave in England, leaving Borton and Smith to continue their reconnaissance to the Far East.

When he returned to Cairo at the beginning of 1919 Salmond found a nasty situation developing. The war with the Turks was over but it looked as though a new one with the Arabs was about to begin. By this time educated Arabs in Cairo were aware of the Balfour Declaration, promising a homeland for the Jews in Palestine. They were also aware that while Sir James McMahon had been promising Sherif Hussein that Arab lands would become independent when the Turks had been driven out, Sir Mark Sykes had been agreeing the very opposite with the French. France was going to have the Lebanon and Syria and Britain was going to have Palestine and Iraq, although nominal Arab kings would be allowed providing that they did as they were told.

Rioting against the British began in Syria once news of Allenby's denial to Prince Feisal of real Arab sovereignty became known and the rioting was not confined to Syria.

In September 1918, with the war nearly over, Egyptians had begun to press for independence along the lines advocated by President Wilson in his Fourteen Points, which had been published in January 1918. Two days after the Armistice the Arab leaders asked the permission of the High Commissioner, Sir Reginald Wingate, to send a delegation (Arabic word *wafd*) to London to press their case. Sir Reginald Wingate refused and on

8 March 1919 the four leaders of the delegation were imprisoned. The next day they were deported to Malta.

Within a week Egypt was paralysed by general strikes. There were widespread riots all over the country and all classes of men and women participated. Telegraph and railway lines were cut, taxi drivers and lawyers refused to work and thousands went on to the streets to demonstrate. Garrisons in isolated places were besieged and there were general strikes in Cairo.

The British General Headquarters for the Middle East was removed from the *Savoy Hotel* in the centre of Cairo to the less vulnerable *Palace Hotel* at Heliopolis where a substantial garrison was based. Emergency RAF operational squadrons were formed, using the staff of those wartime training squadrons that had not yet been disbanded. Schemes of defence for the airfields were prepared and demobilization was temporarily halted. The British tried to quell the rebellion by force and by midsummer more than 800 Egyptians, 31 Europeans and 29 British soldiers had been killed.

Wingate appealed to London to allow the Wafd (the word now became the name of a political party) to attend the Peace Conference and put their case but the Cabinet would not hear of it. The situation was out of control. Eventually Wingate was

Protests in Cairo in March 1919 against the Balfour Declaration. (AWM PO1588-028-1-1)

replaced by General Allenby who no longer had a war to wage. Because of his successful Middle Eastern campaign Allenby had more influence in London than Wingate. The Wafd delegation was allowed to return to Egypt and was given permission to go to Paris. The next day they signed a statement urging the people to stop demonstrating and they set off for Paris on 7 April. Their negotiations were primarily with the British delegation at the Peace Conference and took many months. Britain finally agreed to Egyptian independence in 1922 whilst retaining control of the Sudan and the Suez Canal. A constitution was prepared in 1923 and the leader of the original Wafd delegation became Prime Minister in 1924 although Egypt remained a British protectorate.

In the last year of the war, British forces in Egypt, Palestine and Iraq had been substantially reinforced and more than a quarter of a million troops were stationed there. The experience of the planes working with Allenby, Lawrence and Feisal in the campaign against the Turks, had shown that aircraft were effective in desert warfare. They were much more effective than they had been in Europe where bad weather frequently grounded them. Hiding from aeroplanes in the desert was difficult and once the war was over and the Turks had gone home, there was nothing to oppose British aircraft, either in the air or on the ground.

By early 1919 the Arabs generally knew that Britain had betrayed them. All that they had achieved by helping to clear the Middle East of Turks was to exchange subjugation within the Ottoman Empire for subjugation under the French and the British.

Britain and France had broken promises to the Arabs in order to win the war. But for the arrival of the Americans, the war could have been lost in March 1918 when the Germans were only forty-five miles from Paris. To get the Americans into the war and introduce conscription there, the Jewish lobby in Congress had to be encouraged. President Wilson in his Fourteen Points, which were the starting point for the 1919 Peace Settlement, had advocated self determination for the populations of the Middle East but his closest advisors were Zionists and Balfour had already made his infamous Declaration. Failure to grant independence to the Iraqis after the war is more difficult to justify but is simply explained by the sudden realization of the importance of oil. None of these justifications and explanations had any appeal to the Arabs. They had been cheated of everything; no independence despite fighting for it, and a planned massive influx of Jews into a land that had been theirs for 1,300 years.

The first Arab insurrection against the Jews in Palestine itself did not begin until 4 April 1920. It arose during celebration of the Muslim feast of Nebi Musa, which took place just outside Jerusalem at the reputed site of the tomb of Moses – a patriarch revered by Jews, Christians and Muslims alike. Inopportunely, because it was also the Passover, Jewish youths paraded in favour of a Jewish Defence Force and the Arabs turned on them. The riot spread throughout Old Jerusalem and British Mandate troops lost control. Four Jews were killed and 200 injured.

In Iraq in the autumn of 1920, denial of self government led to the heaviest loss of life in any of the mandated territories. The rebellion there cost about 4,000 Arab lives and 400 British and it took on the character of a jihad led by Shi'a clerics. At one stage the British only retained control in Basra, Baghdad and Mosul and that was due in no small measure to the successful work of the RAF in carrying out punitive bombing raids on rebellious tribes. Winston Churchill, as Secretary of State for Air, advocated the use of poison gas. Writing as President of the Air Council in 1919 he commented:

The beginning of the Muslim feast of Nebi Musa in Jerusalem on 4 April 1920. It marked the outbreak of the first Arab violence against the Jews in Palestine. (Wikipedia)

> I do not understand the squeamishness about the use of gas. I am strongly in favour of using poisonous gas against uncivilised tribes.[1]

The Handley Page bombers with their one-ton payload and mechanized bomb delivery system would have been ideal for this but the Cabinet declined to follow Churchill's suggestion.

National boundaries did not exist. Vast and barren stretches of desert made natural boundaries for the Arabs but they were united by their strongly held religious beliefs and their quest for independence. The rebellion erupted as far south as Luxor in Upper Egypt, as far north as Mosul in Mesopotamia and as far east as Amritsar in India. In Mesopotamia (Iraq) alone it was estimated that there were about 130,000 tribesmen under arms.[2] It spread from the Mediterranean to the Caspian Sea in western Persia (Iran). Afghanistan was also in revolt.[3]

In 1917 and 1918 the techniques of fighting in the desert with the aid of aircraft had been perfected and it was apparent that more planes would be of great benefit. The RAF had built an aeroplane factory at Heliopolis in 1918 but it was only equipped to build fighters and it had no facilities for building bombers. The fighters that were wanted were the latest designs such as the Bristols that had performed so well in the closing stages of the war. The bombers that were needed were the Handley Page O/400s, which were, for the moment, the only ones immediately available. There were plenty of these in France; the problem was how to get them to Egypt. Given time, fighters could be packed in crates and shipped to Alexandria and they could be re-assembled in the factory at Heliopolis. But the Handley Page bombers were a more difficult proposition because of their size, or so it was thought.

Major General Geoffrey Salmond, seeing the rioting that followed the arrest and exile of the four Egyptian Wafd leaders, sent the following message to the Air Ministry in March 1919:

> The experience gained and the lesson taught by the events in Egypt during the last seven weeks clearly indicate the imperative necessity for the permanent maintenance of at least three service squadrons in Egypt, supplemented by 1 or 2 long distance squadrons of the Handley Page type.[4]

Handley Pages were needed because servicing facilities were only available at Heliopolis and the flight to Iraq (Mesopotamia) was beyond the range of other machines except those carrying insignificant bomb loads.

On 17 April he wrote again:

> The general situation is still unsatisfactory. Despite generous concessions on the part of the government, there still seems to be a spirit of unrest which at times assumes the form of violence. Stringent methods have to be adopted to enforce order and clearly aerial patrols are necessary.

About events in Mesopotamia, where the worst rioting took place, he wrote:

> Some of the tribes are not unlike the tribes of the north-west frontier of India in their manner of raiding and fighting in the hills. Consequently our ground forces seldom get in touch with them and RAF work is confined to reconnaissance and bombing. We bombed a tribal chief's village with 20 pound Coopers bombs and obtained 17 direct hits. The next day when we returned, the tents had disappeared and the inhabitants ran out into the desert before bombs could be dropped. Nevertheless 36 bombs were dropped with good results on houses and also on a convoy of camels and donkeys.

Air reconnaissance made surprise attacks by the Arabs on convoys, railways or garrisons difficult. Pilots were trained to watch for clusters of Bedouin tents without accompanying flocks of sheep. They spelt trouble.

So more aircraft were needed and they were needed quickly. The next move was the responsibility of the Air Ministry.

Notes
1. War Office minute, 12 May 1919.
2. Michael Armitage, *The Royal Air Force*, Arms & Armour Press, 1993.
3. Air 1/21/15/1/102, Air 1/35/15/1/226, Air 1/2372/226/7/39.
4. Air 1/21/15/1/102.

CHAPTER 8

At the Air Ministry

The Air Ministry pondered the problem. So far as aeroplanes and the men to fly them were concerned, surely there could be no difficulty. At the end of the war the RAF had in service or in store 22,000 aeroplanes. It also had 267,000 officers and men.

Just before the war ended, the then Chief of the Air Staff, Major General Sir Frederick Sykes, had written a paper for the government in which he foresaw a large fleet of aeroplanes continuing to promote Britain's economic interests and maintain her position as the leading aviation power after the war.[1] This would be the logical continuation of the build-up of the Independent Force, which was intended to bomb Germany in 1919. No one saw that the end of the war was imminent and no one found fault with Sykes' grand plan while the war was still in progress, even though he was thinking of a peacetime air force of sixty-two Service squadrons with a further ninety-two in skeleton form, which could be expanded if the need arose. Of the sixty-two Service squadrons in Sykes' proposal, seventeen would be bomber squadrons and three would be flying boats. He also proposed substantial subsidies to private aircraft manufacturers because he recognized their important role in the future development of aviation. Both before and during the war they had been markedly more successful than the Royal Aircraft Establishment in the design and manufacture of aeroplanes, with names such as Avro, Bristol, Handley Page, Sopwith and Vickers leading the way.

It was in this climate of opinion in the autumn of 1918 that No. 1 Aerial Route RAF between England, France and Egypt came into being *on paper* with Sykes as its sponsor. Ellington's misgivings about the likely casualty rate and the likely duration of each flight were discounted and the earlier assertion by Major General Geoffrey Salmond, Brigadier Groves and Major McLaren that it would be quicker to fly the machines rather than to ship them was accepted. From this moment onward it is important to follow the timing of events because it is a crucial factor in explaining what went wrong.

The sudden end of the war brought a dramatic change in the political situation. There was a general election in December 1918. A Lloyd George coalition of a sort continued. But it was on very different terms with Lloyd George no longer the great war leader that he had been. The war had come close to bankrupting Britain and many of her pre-war assets had been sold to the USA. By 1918 the war was costing £10 million[2] a day and the Air Ministry, aircraft production and the RAF, between them, accounted for a tenth of this. The national debt was fourteen times greater than it had been in 1914 and interest payments on it were absorbing nearly half of all taxation. This could not go on. Lloyd George and Austin Chamberlain, his Chancellor, decreed that military spending had to be reduced to 80 per cent (in real terms) of what it had been in 1914. The cuts were to begin immediately.

In the new government Winston Churchill was appointed Secretary of State for War and, to save on ministerial salaries, Lloyd George asked him to combine with it the duties of Secretary of State for Air. At this stage in his career, despite his early enthusiasm for flying, Churchill's knowledge of aviation was slight and the amount of time that he spent on air matters was minimal. He was obsessed with supporting the White Russians in their campaign against the Bolsheviks. His Under Secretary of State for Air, General Seely, later resigned because he said that Churchill was only devoting one hour per week to air force matters and important issues were being neglected.

Although Frederick Sykes was Chief of the Air Staff he had a lesser reputation than General Trenchard who had been commander of the Royal Flying Corps in France for most of the war and was a staunch supporter of Field Marshal Haig. Trenchard had been appointed Chief of the Air Staff in April 1918 when the RAF was formed but he had rapidly fallen out with Lord Rothermere, the Secretary of State for Air, who despised Haig for

Lord Trenchard. Chief of the Air Staff from 1919 until 1930.

Sir Frederick Sykes. Chief of the Air Staff in 1918.

his pointless waste of soldiers' lives. Being loyal to Haig, Trenchard resigned abruptly only six weeks after being appointed. He was replaced by Sykes.

In February 1919, a fortnight after his appointment as Secretary of State for War and for the Air, Churchill called Trenchard to his office to discuss the RAF's future. Without notifying Sykes, the current Chief of the Air Staff, who was away at the Peace Conference in Paris, Churchill offered Sykes' job to Trenchard and explained that Sykes would be made Director of Civil Aviation as a consolation prize. Churchill showed Trenchard the eighty-three-page Sykes-Air Ministry plan for the post-war RAF, said it was far too expensive, and asked him to prepare a cheaper one. The coalition government was unpopular and after the dreadful loss of life in the war that had just ended, the people were pacifist. Drastic cuts in taxation had had to be made. Lloyd George was even thinking of abolishing the RAF in line with Army and Navy wishes.

Trenchard went away and the same evening he prepared an 800-word paper that provided for drastic cuts in expenditure at the Air Ministry and in the RAF. He made no attempt to consult the Air Ministry since he was not yet officially part of it and, in any case, the two key members, Sir Frederick Sykes and Brigadier P.R.C. Groves, were both away in Paris. Churchill saw no need to discuss Trenchard's plans with Sykes either. He accepted Trenchard's outline proposals on the spot, although they required considerable later elaboration and negotiation of budgets with the Cabinet. They were not published until December 1919 when they appeared as a White Paper presented to Parliament by Churchill.[3] This White Paper provided no money at all for the maintenance or development of bombers such as the Handley Page O/400 and the Vickers Vimy.

The Air Estimates for 1920, prepared in 1919, equalled little more than two weeks of the RAF expenditure incurred in 1918. The planned run-down was:

1918:   £370 million
1919:   £54 million (including compensation for cancelled contracts)
1920:   £17 million (The Sykes plan would have cost about £50 million)

The replacement of Sykes by Trenchard took place on 15 February 1919 and three weeks after he was appointed Trenchard fell seriously ill with Spanish influenza. By the time he had recovered and was at his desk in the Air Ministry in May, drastic cuts in skilled manpower in the RAF had already been made and funds for essential supplies and equipment had been cut off. Numbers in the RAF fell from 267,000 at the end of the war to 150,000 by May 1919 and to 30,000 by the beginning of 1920. In total, 10,000 aeroplanes and 30,000 engines were scrapped. These cuts coincided precisely with the inauguration of No. 1 Aerial Route. The decision to create it had been taken while Sykes was Chief of the Air Staff but its implementation was not now under his control. Indeed it appears that during the months of March and April 1919 it was largely out of anyone's control because of Trenchard's influenza and subsequent pneumonia.

The manpower cuts that took place between November 1918 and May 1919 took no account of the technical skills of the men concerned. The most experienced and therefore most skilled, had longer service than others and they received priority for demobilization. Even when Trenchard returned to work he gave No. 1 Aerial Route a lower priority than his work to build a minuscule air force with a budget of just £17 million. It cannot be

Handley Page bombers waiting to be scrapped after the war. (Chaz Bowyer)

overlooked that in proposing that tiny budget he was securing the position of Chief of the Air Staff for himself in place of his rival Frederick Sykes. Trenchard could have moderated Churchill's request for a dramatic reduction in the RAF budget but he chose not to. At the same time it should be remembered that Churchill regarded membership of the Cabinet, and perhaps being the head of it, as the highest priority in his life. Lloyd George wanted a drastic cut in RAF expenditure. Lloyd George would have it. Lloyd George had been Churchill's guide, mentor and friend since Churchill first arrived in the Commons. Perhaps this was the way to get to the top.

Trenchard had not proposed the Aerial Route but he did not try to countermand the plan to fly Handley Pages to Egypt. Geoffrey Salmond had said that they were urgently needed. So be it. Perhaps Trenchard felt no responsibility for the outcome of a project that had been initiated by his predecessor who was a man for whom he felt personal animosity. In his five months' experience in 1918 as commander of the Independent Force, which was intended to bomb Germany's industrial heartland, he thought that bombers were ineffective. In Trenchard's diary entry for 11 November 1918, in referring to that short episode in his life, he wrote:

> A more gigantic waste of effort and personnel there has never been in any war.[4]

The timing of the change in command from Sykes to Trenchard and the drastic cut in RAF expenditure could not have been more disastrous for the men and machines involved in pioneering the world's first air route. The first aircraft took off from northern France on 3 May 1919 and the last one arrived in Egypt in mid-November.

Notes

1. Memorandum by the Chief of the Air Staff on the Air Power Requirements of the Empire, 12 September 1918.
2. At least £1 billion today. Source – Estimates presented to Parliament on 24 July 1917.
3. The Permanent Organization of the RAF. Cmd. 467.
4. H.M. Hyde, *British Air Policy Between the Wars*. Quoted in the *Dictionary of National Biography*. 2004 edition. It is part of Trenchard's diary entry for 11 November 1918.

CHAPTER 9

'Won't it be Fun if we Come Down Here!'

No more Handley Pages rolled out of the eleven factories that had been making them. The manufacturing contracts were suspended and compensation was negotiated with the suppliers. But shortage of machines for the mass flight to Egypt was not seen as a problem. Borton and McLaren were fortunate to have the benefit of brand-new machines for their flights the previous year but there were still plenty of used ones lying about. Indeed there were eight Handley Page O/400 squadrons based in France, each with two flights of five machines and several machines in reserve. Some had been engaged in strategic bombing and some had been used in tactical support of the army. My father was one of the pilots in 207 Squadron but it is three other squadrons based in France, 58, 214 and 216, which are central to the story that follows.

Despite Ellington's misgivings, Geoffrey Salmond firmly believed that the Handley Pages would get to Cairo more quickly if they flew instead of being shipped. If they followed the usual shipment system, they would have been sent by rail to Marseille and then by ship to Alexandria. This would have taken about four weeks, compared with Geoffrey Salmond's estimate of six days for flying them there. It should be remembered that a squadron consisted of much more than the two flights of five aircraft and the twenty pilots and twenty fitters and riggers that would fly in them. A further two hundred support staff were to be transported by ship as well as their motor vehicles, heavy duty servicing equipment and countless spare parts. The Establishment Book for a Handley Page squadron lists everything from spare Rolls-Royce engines down to the smallest nuts and bolts. A copy is in the National Archive and it has sixty-five pages.[1] I have found no records of the shipment of all these people and their equipment to Cairo. Presumably it caused no problems to the Air Ministry and has therefore left no history. For each squadron it must have taken at least three weeks.

At the same time as the decision to fly the Handley Pages was taken, it was also decided to pack up the Snipes of 80 Squadron, the Bristols of 48 Squadron and the DH9s of 206 Squadron and send them from France to Egypt by ship.[2] So Ellington's remarks about the risks of flying the route had at least some effect. The doubtful privilege of flying to Egypt was reserved for the Handley Pages.

Geoffrey Salmond in Egypt was so anxious to get his reinforcements that planes began flying the route through France and Italy before the staging posts were set up so there was a shortage of adequately skilled maintenance staff.

58 Squadron, which had been stationed at Provin near Lille, was ordered to set off first. It had the normal complement of ten Handley Pages in two flights of five. Captain Henderson commanded C Flight and Captain Dunkerly commanded the other. The Squadron Commander was Major D. Gilley DFC.[3]

The first flight of machines that took off included the plane that was carrying Lawrence as passenger. They left Buc airfield on 3 May then just outside Paris but now close to the Boulevard Périphérique. It took them more than two weeks to get as far as Rome. Because of the need to allow for headwinds, a Handley Page with a full load of petrol had a safe range of only about 400 miles. They had refuelling and servicing stops at Lyon, Marseille and Pisa. With a maximum speed of 100 miles per hour they could only manage one leg of the journey in a day. Significant cloud or strong winds like the mistral could ground them for days at a time. Headwinds could more than halve their effective speed over land and if the engines were run full out for long they would overheat. At each overnight stop the mechanic had to change oiled-up plugs, change petrol filters and clean the carburettors. Sometimes propellers had to be changed for they were easily damaged by hailstones or warped in hot weather. The petrol tanks had to be replenished and for refuelling there was, at best, a hand pump. In some places not even this was available and the job had to be done by hand with a hundred or more jerry cans.

The machine carried a pilot, an observer, who was also the reserve pilot, a mechanic and a rigger. There was just enough room in the rear gunner's cockpit to squeeze in a passenger such as Lawrence. Apart from the heavy Rolls-Royce engines, the petrol tanks and some box girders in the fuselage, the machines were constructed of wooden struts, canvas and hundreds of rigging and control wires. These had to be re-tensioned after every flight and the free running of the pulleys through which the control wires ran had to be ensured. Rust could cause friction. Rigging was a skilled job. The wings could not bear their own weight without the help of the rigging wires. Flapping pieces of loose canvas had to be replaced and glued or sewn into place and damaged areas re-painted with cellulose dope. Handley Pages were large but fragile.

Lawrence was a great admirer of the Handley Page machines. He had flown in D9681 with Ross Smith during the last weeks of the desert campaign the previous year. The machine in which T.E. Lawrence now flew was D5439. All went well until they reached Rome. The flight was so smooth that Lawrence spent some time when the machine was between Paris and Marseille writing the opening chapters of his book. In chapter 2 of Robert Graves' biography of Lawrence, he quotes him, when describing the flight, as saying:

> Its rhythm is unlike the rest. I like the munch, munch, munch of the synchronised Rolls-Royce engines.[4]

But accidents dogged the Squadron from the outset. The first was on 6 May when HP D5434, one of the other machines in this first flight had 'petrol trouble' and made a forced landing near Châlons sur Marne. Unfortunately, the plane hit a tree and had to be written off. The crew was unhurt.

The next serious accident was the fatal crash of D5439 at Centocelle, which was described in the first chapter. Lawrence recovered but he had to wait for a replacement Handley Page to arrive before he could continue his journey. There would be plenty

95

to choose from because those three squadrons were all scheduled to make the journey.

As recommended by Geoffrey Salmond, the Route was placed under the command of Major Stuart McLaren who had been co-pilot on the first flight to Egypt. Because of the perceived urgency, the official inauguration of the Route did not take place until 6 June, a month after planes of 58 Squadron began flying it. McLaren decided to base himself at St Raphael near Marseille and on 7 July he issued standing instructions concerning the establishment and responsibilities of the RAF personnel who were at that moment being posted along the route at the places he had selected.

The stations along the route were each given alphabetic letters from A to K. To begin with, the staffing of some of the airfields was minimal – in some cases just a rigger and two fitters for refuelling and minor repairs with an NCO in charge. Later, in the light of experience, each station had a minimum staff of two officers and several fitters and riggers. The larger stations such as Taranto had many more. At least one of the officers had to be a Handley Page pilot. Their responsibilities were the obvious ones of refuelling, servicing, obtaining spares, providing accommodation for air crews en route, giving them weather forecasts and notifying St Raphael of each machine's progress.

Each station was given a telegraphic address, which was notified to the postal authorities along the route so that pilots who had forced landings could send telegrams for assistance and each staging post had instructions about recovering wrecked planes and salvaging spares from them.

The units principally using the route were the three Handley Page squadrons from France. These were followed by a pool of replacement HPs and six Vickers Vimys. Six of the replacement HPs came from 207 Squadron in which my father had served in France and which was now being disbanded. The rest of the HPs and the six Vickers Vimys came from England, some straight from the manufacturer. The difference in reliability between the machines that came straight from the factory and the machines that had seen service in France in the previous year soon became apparent.

The bases were only established as far as Taranto by 26 July yet most of 58 Squadron had already flown past Taranto and was in

Egypt by 2 July. The first four planes of 214 Squadron were also without support at Taranto and all that was going to arrive of 214 was in Egypt by 2 August. Most of 216 Squadron limped in by the middle of October.

According to Leslie Semple's photograph album, the Suda Bay HP team officers did not arrive until 2 August so they can only have serviced 216 Squadron, the stragglers from the other two, plus most of the 24 reserve HPs and five of the six Vickers Vimys that were added to the plan to compensate for the losses en route. Most of 58 and 214 Squadrons' servicing needs should have been met by the fitters and riggers already at the Suda seaplane base. The GOC RAF Mediterranean had some F3 Flying boats to maintain and these used the same Rolls-Royce engines as the HPs. Men with adequate experience of these engines appear not to have been among those at Suda Bay. Because of sand flies and mosquitoes, Suda Bay was not a popular posting. Proven skilled men had the most bargaining power and they tried to avoid Suda, so technical expertise was concentrated at Malta and Alexandria. Only when troubles developed were Captain Lewis, Lieutenant Semple and five ground crew with HP experience sent out. By then it was too late.

Soon after Lawrence's plane crashed it emerged that McLaren, at Pisa, had omitted to warn the pilots about the pronounced slope of the airfield at Centocelle. Nor was Lawrence's crew warned that sunset at Rome was about an hour earlier than the time that pilots were used to at Lille. A heated row developed between Major Gilley, the CO of 58 Squadron, and McLaren. Gilley objected to McLaren's hustle and to the machines being pushed on to Rome before they had received scheduled maintenance. Three of them had already had forced landings between Paris and Pisa and Gilley was worried for the rest of his men's safety. McLaren on the other hand was anxious to do the bidding of Salmond in Egypt and get the machines there quickly, even if some risk was involved. Gilley stood up to McLaren whereupon McLaren relieved him of his command and sent him back to England. They were both majors but McLaren was in charge of the Route and that made him senior. He appointed Flight Lieutenant Henderson, the Flight Commander of C Flight, as acting Squadron Commander in Gilley's place.

A Handley Page O/400 undergoing scheduled maintenance. This was a major operation. Note that scaffolding boards and trestles have to be used to protect the canvas wings from the mechanics boots. (Q12178)

Henderson never forgave McLaren for his part in what he considered to be the needless loss of Prince and Spratt's lives at Centocelle. Henderson left the Air Force soon after reaching Egypt. He had the right to do this because of the demobilization regulations. Before he left he must have expressed his feelings to his successor, Major I.T. Lloyd, and Lloyd had this to say to the OC of the Training Brigade, Middle East in his official report on 58 Squadron's flight:

> The loss of Major Gilley at Pisa tended considerably to lower the morale of the squadron and I consider that whatever Major McLaren's criticisms of this officer, they did not warrant his being relieved of his command in the middle of the enterprise. The question of policy rested or should have rested entirely in Major Gilley's hands and had it done so I am convinced that Lieut. Prince's and Lieut. Spratt's deaths might have been avoided ... Arrangements for receiving the machines throughout seem to have been carried out in a most cursory manner and this, combined with a series of conflicting orders, by telegram, received by Captain Henderson taxed this officer's initiative to the full.

> ... In conclusion I would like to suggest that for future flights of this kind, adequate financial arrangements should be made before starting as all the officers who took part in this flight were called upon to pay out of their own pockets, excessive charges for food and lodging for themselves and their men.[5]

It was bold of Major Lloyd to speak out in this way. His report was bound to be read by The Air Officer Commanding, Middle East and he was Geoffrey Salmond, the very man who was pressing McLaren to push the machines along regardless. Geoffrey Salmond must have realized that Lloyd got his information from Henderson and Henderson suffered for it later.

In McLaren's defence it needs to be recorded that, at the subsequent enquiry, McLaren claimed that he sacked Gilley because Gilley was a weak manager and his officers took advantage of this, giving rise to an over casual approach to the job in hand.[6] Another view might be that McLaren was a martinet. Certainly he deemed it necessary to send an order to the officers in charge of route stations saying that:

> Pilots be instructed not to send promiscuous telegrams all over the country on arrival at aerodromes. The Officer In Command of the area concerned will send the necessary reports. Pilots are only to send telegrams in the event of a forced landing and then only to the Officer in Command of the area concerned.

Surely this was unreasonable. Since the war had been over for six months there can have been no security risk in letting one's wife or parents know that another leg of the journey had been safely completed. It was dangerous work that they were doing and families at home would have been worried. The previous year when Brigadier Borton flew the route and the war was still raging, his family in Kent were informed *daily* of his progress by the Director of Flying Operations at the Air Ministry, Brigadier General Groves.

After the accident at Centocelle, Lawrence was released from hospital and had a short convalescence at the British Embassy. On 29 May he set off again in another 58 Squadron machine. He was still a sick man but he scrambled into the HP and continued his writing.

Climbing into a Handley Page. Not easy for a man with a cracked shoulder blade, one arm in plaster and sore ribs. (IWM Q28051)

At Otranto they were delayed for an overhaul of the machine and then flew on to Valona on the Albanian coast. Here one of the accompanying machines needed an overhaul and, since they were flying in a group for mutual security, they were all delayed.

> There were no quarters for the pilots or the mechanics and only iron rations were available. What little Italian currency the entire personnel possessed, being at a decided discount in

100

Albania, empty four-gallon petrol tanks, which had been stowed in the machines to help keep them afloat in the event of coming down in the Adriatic, became the medium of exchange. The law of supply and demand soon made itself felt and as soon as all the housewives within walking distance had all the tins they could use, the rate of exchange fell from a dozen eggs and a string of figs to one can to three or four eggs and perhaps a fig or two.[7]

Eventually, all the machines took off again. One had to return to Valona with a broken cam shaft and another had a forced landing near Piraeus but the rest reached Athens where they were greeted by the King of Greece. Some comic relief was afforded because there were two airfields not far apart and the squadron landed at the wrong one. The King dashed to this airfield but by the time he arrived the planes had taken off for the other airfield. Lawrence, who enjoyed poking fun at dignity, was highly amused.

While awaiting the stragglers at Athens, they took Greek officers for joyrides and Lawrence showed Henderson, the newly appointed 58 Squadron Commander, the principal archaeological sites. Lawrence had seen them before the war. Then they continued to Suda Bay, which they reached on 15 June. Most of the other flight arrived two days later. After landing on Crete it was discovered that one machine had both propellers cracked and that two of the cylinders on one engine were damaged.

Lying peacefully at its moorings in the bay was a large America IV flying boat. The pilot was in hospital with sand fly fever so the problem of spare propellers and exhaust valve springs was soon solved. With no one from the seaplane base about, the newly arrived fitters cannibalized it. Although for use with the same Rolls-Royce Eagle VIII engines as the Handley Pages, the propellers were metal tipped and of a much heavier pitch than those fitted to Handley Pages. But when fitted, the repaired Handley Page with a minimum load just managed to stagger into the air.

While repairs were in progress at Suda Bay, Lawrence filled in the time by exploring the palace at Knossos, which had been excavated by Arthur Evans in the early 1900s. Knossos is seventy miles east of Suda Bay and was by this time famous for Arthur Evans' discoveries there of the remains of the Minoan civilization and the Linear A and B scripts – forerunners of Greek.

The Palace at Knossos. (T.E. Lawrence)

On 21 June, while Lawrence was sightseeing on Crete, HP F318 set off from RAF Kenley in Kent. Like Borton's machine a year earlier, it was brand new and straight from the factory. Its mission was to carry a VIP passenger, H. St John Philby, to Cairo. He was an India Office diplomat and he was being sent to mediate between Sherif Hussein and Ibn Saud who was Hussein's geographical neighbour and territorial rival in the eastern half of Arabia.[8]

The crew comprised Lieutenants H.A. Yates and J.D. Vance with mechanics Stedman and Hand. Because Philby was urgently required in Cairo, the crew decided to attempt to beat Borton's record by flying the whole journey in three days. They left England on 21 June and arrived in Paris that afternoon. Next day they flew on to Lyon where they were obliged to refuel the aircraft themselves. Despite that they flew on to Marseille where they punctured two tyres while landing. They mended the tyres, refuelled and flew on to Pisa the same day. The next day they reached Rome and then Taranto. To reach the toe of Italy in less than three days was good going.

They set off for Suda Bay, Crete, next morning but found that their starboard petrol pump was not working. This meant that the starboard engine could not receive petrol from the main tank in the fuselage. They diverted to Athens, which was one hour's flying time closer than Suda Bay, but they couldn't make it and were obliged to land in a partially dry river bed beside the Gulf of Corinth. The landing was skilful in rocky terrain but even so they punctured one tyre and broke the tail skid. They transferred petrol from the fuselage tank to the starboard wing tank, mended the puncture and with the help of local inhabitants, who lifted the tail off the ground, mended the tail skid. From the Gulf of Corinth they flew the last stretch to Athens with the mechanics hand pumping petrol all the way.

At Athens they were delayed for ten hours because the petrol supplied contained water and they had to empty all the tanks and strain the petrol through chamois leather. They left for Crete next day, hand pumping all the while. En route for Crete the port propeller split in the air setting up a violent vibration but they managed to maintain enough height on one engine to scrape into Suda Bay on the 25th and make a safe landing. Another flying boat propeller was 'borrowed' and Lawrence and Philby now flew together for the last part of the journey.

No advance arrangements had been made with the seaplane base at Suda to house and feed the crews and no one, apart from a few mildly interested olive growers, came near the machines. But just as the flight was about to leave on 29 June a sailor turned up on a bike bearing a 'signal' from the Senior Naval Officer at the seaplane base, asking why the arrival of the machines had not been reported. This was taken to Colonel Lawrence, who was the senior officer in the Handley Page party and he finally agreed to frame a reply. It was typical of him. He wrote a full foolscap page asking the Senior Naval Officer where he had been hiding. Within sight of the cannibalized flying boat, the senior RAF officer present (Henderson) suggested that perhaps an explanation and a formal apology to the Senior Naval Officer would be more appropriate but T.E. Lawrence insisted on his message as it was – or nothing.

Lawrence's reaction is not unreasonable. The photograph of Brigadier Borton's machine arriving over the airfield the previous summer was taken from the seaplane base. This shows that it would have been difficult for the arrival of the 58 Squadron planes not to have been noticed at the Suda Naval Base only two miles away. One may suppose that the naval base knew that it lacked the expertise to give practical assistance and decided to keep out of the way. The RAF personnel for the airfield were still in transit from England.

A single flying boat arrived to provide escort on 24 June but as not all the Handley Pages were yet ready to fly and several of the crews were in hospital at Suda Bay with sandfly fever, the escort returned to Alexandria.

Sandfly fever is a viral infection that is carried by infected sand flies that bite the victim. The flies can penetrate mosquito nets and the only preventative action is to impregnate the netting with a heavy dose of insecticide. The symptoms nowadays do not seem as bad as they were in 1919. The patient suffers from headaches, fever, nausea, back ache and conjunctivitis but usually recovers in about a week.

The flying boat eventually returned to Suda and on 29 June nine planes set off on the flight to Mersah Matruh. But the escort flying boat now found itself unable to rise from the water. Two of the machines flew on ahead without escort and these carried Lawrence, Philby and Captain Henderson.

In a later memoir Captain Henderson, recalled:

> During the crossing, when all signs of land and shipping had disappeared, T.E. pushed a note into my hand 'Won't it be fun if we come down here? I don't think![9]

The hospital at Suda Bay where the sandfly victims lay, looked after by European nurses. (LGS)

Lawrence recognized the danger involved in sending so many planes and crews over the Mediterranean. It had only been achieved by three aeroplanes before and now fifty were attempting it.

The rest of the squadron followed three days later with a replacement escort. Lawrence and Philby were last seen by Captain Henderson disappearing into *Shepheard's Hotel* in Cairo, a lavish building that only the elite and the officer class could enter. It features in David Lean's film *Lawrence of Arabia*, which is better at providing dramatic scenes in the desert than it is at recounting reliable history.

Philby shared with Lawrence his disillusion with British foreign policy as it affected the Arabs. They knew one another well. Philby had been head of the political mission from the India Office to the Arabs in Mesopotamia, in parallel with Sir Henry McMahon in Cairo and like Lawrence he had come to know well the leading Arabs in Mesopotamia. Philby and Lawrence were both strongly anti-Zionist and identified themselves with the Arabs by frequently wearing Arab costume. They were a couple of dissidents together and the journey gave them a chance to dwell on their misgivings.

Handley Page O/400s flying in formation. (Q12186)

105

Shepheard's Hotel in Cairo before its destruction during the riots that deposed King Farouk in 1952. (Brooklyn Museum Archives)

Their particular grievance at the time, apart from the Balfour Declaration, was the way in which, at the Paris Conference, the Arabs were put under pressure to accept a French protectorate in Syria, which was the state that Prince Feisal had been promised. Feisal was later made puppet King of Iraq under a British protectorate. This may have mollified him but it did nothing for Arab aspirations. Lawrence walked out of the 'establishment' and became a superficially anonymous airman. In 1921, under pressure, Philby resigned his British (Indian) Government post as Advisor to the Minister of the Interior in Iraq[10] because he disagreed with British policy. He settled in Jeddah, became a Muslim and played an important part in US negotiations for oil concessions in what later became Saudi Arabia. He was detained at Karachi in 1940, under Regulation 18b, while trying to escape to the USA and he was described in his *Times* obituary as 'not always cantankerously anti-British'.

His eldest son, Kim, at the impressionable age of eighteen, went up to Trinity College Cambridge in 1929, the year before his father became a Muslim. He was joined there the following year by Guy Burgess and the following year again by Donald Maclean. In 1933 there was a communist take-over of the Cambridge University

H. St John Philby with his Arab bodyguard in Mesopotamia. (Q59411)

Socialist Society while the young Philby was still openly a communist.

Kim applied to join the Foreign Office in the autumn of 1933 but was turned down because a reference from Sir Dennis Robertson, a leading Cambridge economist and young Philby's tutor at Trinity College, suggested that he was 'too far left'. So he went to Vienna and was recruited as a Soviet spy instead. He then built himself a 'cover' identity by working as an apparent pro-Fascist journalist covering the Spanish Civil War. Philby, Burgess and Maclean all insinuated themselves into MI5 in due course. The Civil Service Commissioners of the 1930s accepted a public school and Oxbridge background as proof of integrity and loyalty and evidence to the contrary seems not to have registered with them.[11]

Kim Philby.

This is almost the last we hear of Lawrence of Arabia. His path had crossed Borton's in 1918 in Palestine and their paths crossed again when Borton was Commanding Officer at RAF Cranwell in the 1920s and Lawrence was masquerading as 'Aircraftman Shaw' at the same place.

Now let us return to No. 1 Aerial Route RAF and follow the correspondence, which reflects what had been happening along the route.

On 19 May Brigadier Game, the Director of Training and Organization for the RAF had been obliged to report to Trenchard, now Chief of the Air Staff and just out of his sick bed:

> Things are going badly (for 58 Squadron) the squadron being now distributed as under:-
>
> 1 machine   Rome OK
> 1 machine   Rome crashed 2 officers killed
> 6 machines Istres (Marseille)
> 1 machine   Avignon
> 1 machine   Buc (Paris) replacement for the crash
>
> The first flight started on May 3rd – a fortnight ago. Two more squadrons are to follow and I feel sure we shall take months getting them through unless we have an officer to push them along at each aerodrome. McLaren is trying to do this from Rome but pilots take little or no notice of his wires and I have little doubt spend a few days at any pleasant place they stop at.[12]

More criticism arrived from Lieutenant Colonel Reginald Cooper, the British Air Attaché in Rome, in a letter to the Air Ministry following the fatal crash at Rome.

> There seems to have been a great lack of proper management and control throughout. For instance a whole flight was hung up at Lyon because one pilot had been stung on his seat by a wasp and they were all kept back until he could sit up again. Two machines taxied into one another while getting off at Lyon. They have apparently had a great deal of petrol feed trouble. Flights have only been allowed to proceed in fours

'Two machines taxied into one another.' (LGS)

instead of twos or threes. It would have been better if they
had flown in pairs, making short flights in the mornings
only so that the mechanics could go over the machines in
the afternoon. As it is they set off late with the result that the
mechanics have to spend the next day getting the machines
ready again.[13]

The Air Ministry referred the comment 'lack of proper management and control' to the GOC RAF in France and Germany, Major
General John Salmond. He was Geoffrey's younger brother but
had learned to fly the year before him. He was therefore senior to
him. He quickly responded:

McLaren reports directly to the Air Ministry. I have no
responsibility for him. IF I am called upon to take responsibility I will do so but it will be organised on a sound basis.
I suggest that McLaren is recalled for consultation before
sending 214 or 216. Meantime I am cancelling these moves
out of my control pending your further instructions.

Evidently John Salmond was concerned about the ill-prepared-
ness of the route. He was, however, assured that he would not be
held responsible for anything that went wrong after the machines
had left France.[14] This may have been reassuring for him but
not for the airmen involved and it does not absolve him from

responsibility for the well-being of the machines and crews while they were in France. More than half the machines that crashed came down in France and the contrast between the performance of the machines that came straight from factories in England and those that had seen active service in the last stage of the war in France was striking. John Salmond was responsible for the maintenance of the machines based in France.

On 24 May the officer in charge at Istres (Marseille) reported to the Air Ministry:

> There has been much uncertainty about everything to do with the Handley Page aircraft coming into this area. McLaren doesn't keep us informed. There are two machines at Istres awaiting orders. The machines are out in the open because there are no hangars big enough. The intense heat is damaging the propellers and the supports.

The effect of the heat was bad enough but the effect of the mistral gales, which arose frequently in Provence in the summer, was even worse. Yet Istres was in John Salmond's area of responsi-

A Handley Page O/400 in a canvas Bessoneau hangar. These hangars could be erected by twenty men in two days and, provided they were thoroughly pegged down with steel cables and pickets, they were effective protection against gales and rain. (RAF P1607)

Bessoneau hangar being erected. From a model in the Air Museum at Le Bourget, Paris. (CS)

bility and in Northern France, with the war over, he had literally hundreds of redundant Bessoneau hangars that could have been sent by train to Istres and elsewhere along the route. With a trained crew of twenty men each hangar took just two days to erect.[15]

Presumably, Brigadier Game did consult McLaren. It had begun to dawn on him that insufficient preparations for the flights had been made and he decided upon reinforcements.

Director of Training and Organisation to Director of Personnel –

Major McLaren to remain IC at Marseille. Captain Gilmour to Rome.

Officers to be posted to Lyon, Istres, Pisa and Grottaglie. A clerk and orderly to be found for Major McLaren. It is estimated that 6 machines per month will fly the route for the whole of the summer season so 6 specialist crews comprising 2 pilots, 1 Rolls Royce fitter and 1 Handley Page rigger will be required. These crews can be obtained by breaking up the HP V1500 group at present at Bircham Newton.

The appointment of Captain Gilmour to Rome indicates that this staging post is now regarded as a key one. Gilmour was one of the experienced flight commanders from the old 207 Squadron.

On 27 May Brigadier Game estimated that a further sixteen officers, twenty fitters, seven riggers, four NCO storekeepers and six storekeepers were going to be required to man the route stations – many more than originally foreseen – and he received the immediate rejoinder that it would be impossible to collect these personnel together before the second week of June.[16]

Another blow fell at the end of May with the news that the seaplane base at Suda was to be closed at the end of July as part of the post-war economies. The Navy stated that it would be quite impossible to provide a destroyer escort across the Mediterranean, as they had for General Borton's proving flight, so an escort of F3 flying boats based at Malta was proposed instead. This never fully materialized and most machines made the trans-Mediterranean flight to Mersah Matruh without escort.

58 Squadron received conflicting information about the route they were to follow. At various stopping places there were insufficient spares and they had to rely upon Italian generosity to get by. At Pizzone (Taranto) on 9 June the OC 66 Wing RAF refused to get involved in the developing muddle.

> On leaving Rome 58 Squadron were told that an intermediate airfield between Taranto and Athens would be available. But nobody knows where it is. I have suggested that Valona might be suitable but I refuse to take responsibility for the squadron's further movements. I do not know when the squadron is likely to proceed or by which route they may be travelling. They have inspected the Valona airfield and are not pleased. It is really no more than an airstrip for scout machines.

On 16 June the AOC Malta wrote to the Air Ministry

> I cannot provide escort flying boats. Only one pilot is fit for work and he and one other have been waiting around to do the escort work since April 12th. The flying boats have deteriorated in that time. One cannot get off the water. We must have more spares and more repair staff.

This remark serves to illustrate the fragility of these lightly built aeroplanes. The doped canvas covering sagged in the heat and tightened up again when wet and this caused distortion. If a machine was out in a strong wind it usually needed substantial re-rigging before it could fly again.

The shortage of flying boats at Malta was aggravated because a proposal to build more in the Malta dockyard had foundered owing to confusion over whether the expenditure involved should come from the Treasury vote for the Admiralty (RNAS) or the newly formed RAF. The extra flying boats were never built.[17]

On June 20 Major McLaren complained to the Air Ministry that mail arriving by the military airmail service was taking three weeks whereas the civil post took only three days. He also complained that a proposal to base seaplanes at Taranto was nonsense because the longest oversea flight between there and Suda Bay was only fifty miles. They were needed at Suda Bay for the 400-mile leg to Mersah Matruh.

Notes

1. Air 1/32/15/9/133, Air 1/696/21/20/207.
2. Air 1/1011/204/5/1336.
3. Air 2/113/A29664, Air 1/1012/204/5/1319.
4. Robert Graves, *T.E. Lawrence to his Biographer*.
5. Air 2/70/A6347.
6. Major Gilley had earlier been awarded the DFC.
7. David Garnett (ed.) *The Letters of T.E. Lawrence*. Spring Books. London 1964 and Air 2/110/A20872.
8. Ibn Saud eventually won control of Hussein's territory, hence Saudi Arabia.
9. Jeremy Wilson, *The Authorised Biography of T.E. Lawrence*, Heinemann, 1989.
10. It was at about this time that Mesopotamia began to be called Iraq.
11. *Times* obituary of St John Philby who died on 30 September 1960 and Rufina Philby – *The Private Life of Kim Philby*. St Ermin's Press 1999.
12. Air 2/107/A17762.
13. Air 1/1011/204/5/1315.
14. Air 2/107/A17762.
15. Air 1/1117/204/5/2029.
16. Air 1/965/204/5/1085.
17. Air 1/649/17/122/408.

CHAPTER 10

Disaster over Mont St Victoire

On 25 June the Director of Training and Organization, Brigadier Game, who was responsible for the management of No. 1 Aerial Route, sent another message for reinforcements to GOC RAF Halton:

> Lt. L.G. Semple has been appointed for Suda under Captain Charles A. Lewis. He will not be able to obtain a passage before July 5th so he has been sent on leave.

Charles Lewis' appointment was a likely one. From his personnel record he appears to have learned to fly the O/400 at Netheravon in the summer of 1918 and his record states that he had 150 hours' experience of night flying, most of it presumably in the Handley Page. He spent most of May 1919 at the Vickers works at Weybridge learning to fly the Vickers Vimy, which was just coming into service.

The appointment of my father, Leslie Semple, was also appropriate. He had by now more than a year's experience of flying Handley Pages, which, by the standards of the time, was a lot, and he had a good reputation as a pilot. On his very first night bombing sortie in France, he and his crew missed their way home and ended up making a forced landing in an unlit field way past their base and almost on the Channel coast. Peasants rushed up with pitchforks and threatened to kill them until they were satisfied that they were English. When that was sorted out they were taken to a farmhouse and given a hot meal. They stayed with their hosts until dawn and then took off from the field and flew back to their base. 207 Squadron had, hours before, given them up as lost over enemy territory.

Semple also knew personally most of the aircrew in 214 Squadron. While still in France the officers of 214 Squadron spent Christmas Day 1918 in the mess of 207 Squadron and he stayed in their mess for a fortnight when he rescued someone else's Handley Page bogged down in a muddy turnip field in January 1919.[1] He also probably knew some of the 216 Squadron officers because 207 shared with them the Marquise to Merheim airmail service for the Army of Occupation in the Rhineland in the spring of 1919 and the pilots stayed in each other's messes between flights. More significantly, he was a relatively late recruit into the Service and had signed on for an extra year in return for a promise of a grant to go to university when he was eventually demobilized. That university place was the making of his later career and he could not have afforded it without government assistance.

At the time of his appointment to the job, Semple was given the unenviable task of flying the Handley Pages on the oversea leg of the journey from Suda Bay to Mersah Matruh, returning to Suda Bay each time by sea. Fortunately for him, by the time he reached Suda Bay it had been discovered that there was no ferry service between North Africa and Crete and so the idea was impracticable. So from Taranto onwards pilots stayed with their machines all the way to Cairo. The escorting flying boats were mostly mythical and even when they did appear, could not carry passengers in the first half of the crossing because of the large amount of petrol they had to carry at take-off. This serves further to illustrate the lack of adequate planning before the aerial route was launched.

At about this date the route was confirmed as:

Paris (Buc)	A
Lyon	B
Marseille (Istres)	C
Pisa	D
Rome (Centocelle)	E
Barletto	F
Taranto (Pizzone)	G (Instead of Otranto)

Athens (Dekelia)	H
Suda Bay	I
Mersah Matruh	J
Heliopolis	K

These are only the planned stopping places. Many emergency landing and refuelling airstrips, such as Sollum, were designated giving a total of forty-three possible stops on the route.[2]

On 30 June a problem developed over accommodation for the staging post staff at Rome. The Italian Government refused to allow them to be based at the airfield on the grounds that it might set an undesirable international precedent. Debate about this between the British Air Attaché in Rome and the Italian Government continued throughout the summer and badly upset the forward planning of the flights. The Italians offered to service the Handley Pages themselves but the RAF made it abundantly clear that only Rolls-Royce trained fitters could do the job. Eventually, the Italians gave way because they wanted reciprocal facilities at the British airbase at Heliopolis to assist their colonial ambitions in Tripolitania (Libya).

On that same day Geoffrey Salmond advised the Air Ministry that there was only one flying boat at Suda Bay and that it was of doubtful quality. He urged the Air Ministry to put pressure on the Navy to supply an alternative. The Air Ministry tried but the Navy refused. Perhaps pique at the loss of the RNAS to the RAF was involved. Relations between the Admiralty and the newly formed RAF were not good. But overriding everything was the necessity for a huge cut in expenditure by all three services. Meanwhile, flights were delayed.

On 1 July, a telegram from Major McLaren to the Air Ministry pleaded for more time to prepare:

> It is impossible to take delivery of any more machines until my personnel have arrived at their destinations. I will wire you immediately the relay system is ready to function.

At this date it was decided to discontinue Centocelle as the Rome staging airfield and to use Capua instead, which was larger. It had a better surface and did not pose the landing problems that had caused Lawrence's machine to crash on 17 May. A few days later Geoffrey Salmond was expressing concern about the size of fuel tanks for the Suda Bay to Mersah Matruh flight and proposing larger tanks for 214 and 216 Squadrons to guard against headwinds.

The standard fuel tanks on a Handley Page O/400 carried fuel for ten hours' flying. Its maximum speed, with the engines not quite full out, was around 85mph but this was at 1,000–2,000 feet. At 10,000 feet it was only 65mph and there were many mountains of 8,000 feet along the route. How far one travelled on a tankful of petrol therefore depended both on the wind and the height at which the aeroplane was flying. In his diary for 1918 my father recorded a return flight from a night raid in a 60mph headwind in which his Handley Page was flying at an overland speed of only 10mph. In those conditions full tanks would only have taken him 100 miles.[3]

On 3 July HP D4591 left Buc in the company of two others of 214 Squadron. It was delayed at Istres (Marseille) for a complete overhaul but started again on 8 July. Once again it returned with engine trouble but left again next day. It developed engine trouble yet again, within less than an hour, and while the pilot was looking for somewhere to land, stalled while banking at only a few hundred feet and spiralled into a field of lucerne at Pourcieux, east of Aix-en-Provence. See colour photo. It caught fire on impact and all four of the crew were killed. Farm labourers working nearby, who witnessed the stall and the crash, could not get near it for the heat. The crew are buried in the War Graves Commission cemetery at Mazargues, six kilometres from Marseille.

Lieutenant Clifford Hall, one of the pilots, was six days past his twentieth birthday. He came from St Anne's on Sea and his parents inscribed his headstone 'Loved by all who knew him'.[4] The other pilot, Lieutenant Francis Sumner, was an old boy of Tonbridge School. He had joined the RNAS as soon as he was eighteen and, like my father, had learned to fly at Vendome before going to Stonehenge to learn to fly the Handley Page in the summer of 1918.[5]

Corporal Jaffa, at thirty, was the oldest member of the crew. He had been conscripted into the army in 1916 and trained as a rigger in the RFC. In civilian life he had been a cabinetmaker in Whitechapel and he left a widow, Annie.[6] Corporal Elton Flintoft

The cemetery at Mazargues, south-east of Marseille where the crew is buried. (CS)

The pilots' graves at Mazargues. The pilots were only nineteen and twenty and yet they were sent to pioneer this long distance flight from France to Egypt. (CS)

118

The graves of the fitter and the rigger at Mazargues. (CS)

was the aircraft mechanic. Despite the wording on his headstone he was two years older than the pilots and also came from the East End.[7]

Stalling while banking at low altitude was a major cause of fatalities throughout the war. It accounted for a third of all fatal accidents and accidents killed more pilots than enemy action. The lift achieved by a wing depends upon its aerofoil shape being presented to the air passing over it in such a way that the lift it creates is sufficient to counteract gravity. The further the wing moves out of the horizontal, the weaker the lift. Handley Pages were fitted with an instrument called a clinometer in the cockpit. This was a curved spirit level with warning markings on it to show the maximum amount of banking that should be attempted. Why the pilot, Lieutenant Sumner, attempted to bank too steeply in this case we shall never know but his engines had failed and he was anxiously looking for somewhere to land. The danger of overbanking was well known as this extract from an account by a 207 Squadron pilot, Leslie Blacking, shows:

I remember this big bomber chiefly for the heaviness of its controls and the height of its cockpit above the ground. It had to be flown all the time and it was particularly heavy on lateral control. When you put bank on it didn't respond at once. When it did you had to reverse the joystick wheel immediately to take the bank off, and if you went over 45 degrees you were in trouble.[8]

It had been discovered by Dr F.A. Lindemann that when an aeroplane stalls while banking it commences to fall like a stone with one wing leading, and then begins to spin. Providing that there is enough altitude, and provided that the pilot keeps his head, all he has to do is to set his joystick and rudder bar to neutral and let go of them. The machine will come out of the spin and into a shallow glide. Lindemann found this out by doing it, which was brave because he was by no means an expert pilot. It made his name and he became Lord Cherwell, Churchill's senior scientific advisor in the next war. Unfortunately, Lieutenant Sumner was already too low to follow Lindemann's advice.

On 7 July there is evidence of more behind-the-scenes criticism from Lawrence. He had arrived in Cairo a week before and had not been impressed with the organization of the Aerial Route.

AOC RAF Middle East to Air Ministry

Aerial maps were apparently not supplied to 58 Squadron when flying from Paris to Egypt. I understand from Colonel Lawrence that, had the pilots been supplied with aerial maps, the fatal accident to the HP at Rome would almost certainly have been avoided. Also, although there are emergency landing grounds all over Italy our pilots have no maps showing where they are. I consider that immediate steps should be taken to ensure that aerial maps are supplied to 214 and 216 Squadrons. After Sollum we will supply aerial maps for Egypt.

Along No. 1 Aerial Route morale was not good. The war was over and men wanted to return to civilian life. Those along the Route that qualified for demobilization, that is to say the ones with the longest service and therefore greatest experience, began to insist on it.

The area demanded by Hussein and his tribal partners in Syria and Iraq as a reward for driving the Turks out of the Middle East. Palestine was then a province of Syria. (*George Antonius*)

The map agreed between Georges-Picot and Sykes about future control of the Middle East. The area surrounded in blue was to go to the French and the red area including southern Iraq was to go to the British. Palestine, which was a part of Syria, was also to go to the British but with some French participation. (*George Antonius*)

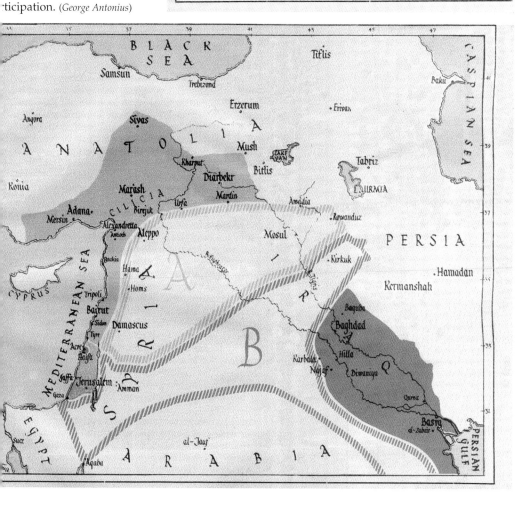

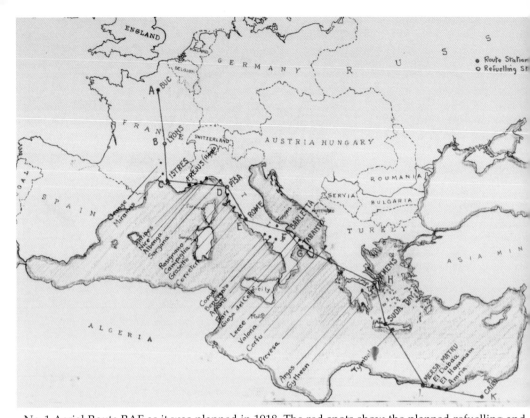

No. 1 Aerial Route RAF as it was planned in 1918. The red spots show the planned refuelling and servicing points and the black spots are proposed emergency landing strips. (*Air 2/113*)

The St Paolo cemetery, just outside the walls of Rome where Lieutenants Prince and Spratt are buried a hundred yards from Shelley's ashes. Their Commonwealth War Graves Commission headstones share a plot (centre of this photograph). (*CS*)

e Australian Light Horse during their epic advance from Romani to Damascus. (*H. Septimus Power, M Art 03647*)

anciful painting by Stuart Reid. The Arabs usually rode camels not horses but it makes a pretty ture. I have not been able to trace the owner of the copyright of this painting.

The fields near Pourcieux where machine D4591 crashed. Mont St Victoire, in the background, wa not the delight for them that it had been for Cézanne. It was banking to avoid this mountain that caused the crash. (CS)

The hilltop cemetery at Monterosso al Mare where Collinge was buried for fifty-five years. Red ro‹ in Monterosso town can just be seen left centre. The photograph shows that the only place to land was indeed the sea. (CS)

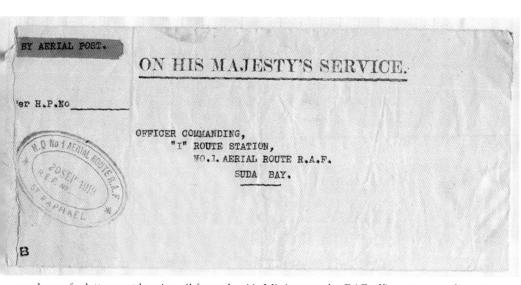

e envelope of a letter sent by airmail from the Air Ministry to the RAF officer commanding at
da Bay. My father stuck it in his scrap book but without any further description or note about the
ntents. It could have been sent to Captain Lewis or to my father if Captain Lewis had already left
England. It is important because it proves that the London to Cairo route was the real No. 1
rial Route RAF and not the route from Cairo to India as other RAF historians like to suggest.

e long gradual approach to the low point in the mountainous spine of the island. To be able to
ke this approach gradually while heading south was a valuable saving of fuel. Those Handley
ges that climbed directly over the mountain range had to spend half an hour circling over Suda
y before they had climbed sufficiently to get over the mountains. *(CS, 2000)*

The goat track that, on Lewis &
Semple's advice, the Vimy
followed through the
mountains. It was this route th
Allied troops followed on thei
retreat to Hora Sfakion in May
1941. The stones in the bottom
left hand corner are the
embankment of the new road.
(*CS, 2000*)

The envelope, with the Vicker:
Vimy overstamping by Ross
Smith and the Australian
postage stamp and cancellatio
which was applied to it when
Ross Smith handed it in at
Brisbane for onward delivery.
is this Brisbane postmark and
cutting from the *Townsville
Bulletin* that prove that it was
the first airmail letter from
Europe to be delivered to the
recipient in Australia. (*CS*)

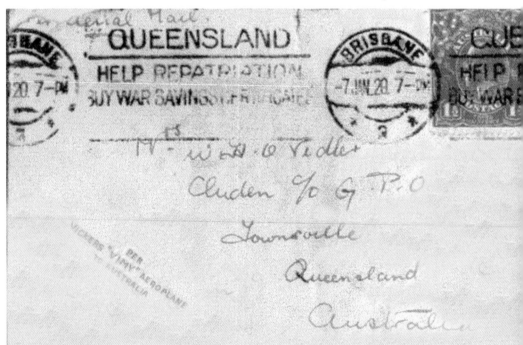

The goat track through the mountain pass has now been superseded by the red road to Hora Sfakion. The altitude markings show that the Vimy could get through the pass at 1,500 metres with about 200 metres to spare.
(© Geographics Chania, Crete)

e route flown between
iro and the Persian Gulf.
rton)

The statue of the crew outside the Vimy museum.
(*Optical Design*)

The statue of Ross Smith in Creswell Gardens, Adelaide.
(*Optical Design*)

Notes

1. 214 Squadron began life as one of the flights of No. 7 Squadron RNAS and was given the number 14. When the RAF was formed all RNAS squadrons had 200 added. Hence 207 and 214.
2. Air 1/1012/204/5/1317.
3. Clive Semple, *Diary of a Night Bomber Pilot in WW1*, p.233.
4. Clifford Hall, 16 The Square, St Anne's on Sea. Born 3.7.1899.
5. Francis Cyril Sumner. Inversnaid, Upper Park Road, Bromley, Kent. Born 20.6.1899.
6. Louis Hyman Jaffe. 1 Spital Street, Whitechapel. Born 1888.
7. Elton Humphreys Flintoft. 5 Grove Green, Leyton. Born 1897.
8. Quotation taken from Chaz Bowyer op. cit.

CHAPTER 11

'All my Staff are Anxious to Get Demobbed'

When No. 1 Aerial Route was first planned it was expected that the squadrons would all have arrived in Egypt by July. It was eight months since the armistice had been signed and seven months since demobilization had begun. After a lunatic 'last in first out' policy had caused a mutiny among the troops at Calais, and a demonstration on Horse Guards Parade, Churchill, as the newly appointed War Minister and Secretary of State for Air, came to the rescue. He introduced new rules that gave men the right to immediate demobilization if they had long service, three wound stripes, or were over thirty-seven. There was also a mutiny among 5,000 soldiers in a Customs shed at Southampton. Trenchard, alone, quelled this by sheer force of personality and by listening to their grievances. Certain men, whose skills were needed at home, such as coal miners, were also allowed to leave. The rules applied to all three services and the rate of demobilization soared. This improved servicemen's morale but led to an exodus from the RAF of men whose expertise was vital.

At the end of the war there were three and a half million in the services. By the end of the summer of 1919 80 per cent of these had been demobilized, in line with the Government's stringent economies.

The Air Ministry – without a boss because Sykes had been fired and Trenchard was too ill to take up his appointment – soon realized that it was losing too many fitters and riggers and in February began inviting such men to re-apply for service in the Air Force. The recruiting drive was not successful. There was a short-lived post-war boom in the British economy and skilled workmen could easily find better jobs.

The following is from a private letter from Major McLaren to the Air Ministry on 14 July, a fortnight after the signing of the Peace Treaty in Versailles.

> Peace has been signed and all my staff are anxious to get demobbed. This place is deadly dull and although I have enough work to keep me occupied I can see that there is dissatisfaction among the men. All the most competent want to be demobilised and get home to their wives or girl friends.
>
> PS Sergeant Quayle is competent. I shall be sorry to lose him. He would stay on as a civilian if the screw were right. What is the policy?
>
> PPS What about my transport driver, my adjutant or secretary and my Bristol fighter?

Following representations from the 58 Squadron pilots, changes were made to the staging posts. The Air Ministry had asked McLaren for a report on an emergency refuelling airfield at Kotiki on the Albanian coast. Back came the reply:

> There is no aerodrome at Kotiki. Perhaps you mean Kourtessi. The French had a squadron based there which averaged one death daily from sandfly fever until they quit. We must use Valona.

Istres was replaced by Fréjus, Capua was confirmed as replacing Centocelle and Foggia was omitted as a refuelling station. It was also confirmed that crews would fly the whole way to Heliopolis instead of having ferry pilots for the oversea journey. This is the decision that saved my father from the job of flying across the Mediterranean regularly. He kept a daily diary while he was at Suda Bay but sadly it was lost when the attic was cleared after his death and we do not know what flying he did while at Suda. From his photographs, he evidently did some.

On 16 July Handley Page D5418 of 216 Squadron was caught on the ground by a whirlwind at Istres. Despite being securely moored with twelve full cans of petrol on each wing and sixteen more on the tail, the machine was blown 200 yards backwards from its moorings into the wall of a hangar and completely wrecked. F305, standing beside it, was lifted several feet off the ground and so badly damaged that it had to stay at Istres until new wings could be obtained from northern France.

Trouble with the Arabs in the Middle East continued and on 17 July the Air Ministry notified McLaren that, in addition to the three squadrons, they were now planning to send a further twenty-four Handley Pages to Egypt and that they hoped the whole operation would be complete by the end of September. This crossed in the wires with a telegram from McLaren:

> Efficiency of route stations is being seriously impaired. Practically all delay in despatch of machines is due to lack of transport. Tenders for Istres and Lyon are urgently required … If I can't have a Bristol fighter, what about an F3 (flying boat) based at Fréjus together with a pilot, 2 fitters and a rigger?

The answer from the Air Ministry was:

> No! But you can have a Bristol fighter.

D4581 of 214 Squadron at Istres. It arrived safely at Heliopolis on 22 July. (Bowyer)

Major McLaren's Bristol on the airfield at Suda Bay. (LGS)

And he appears to have got it. It was promised for mid-August, along with a fitter, and despatched on 3 September.

On 21 July McLaren sent the following telegram. It is optimistic, perhaps because of the good news he had received about having his own Bristol fighter.

> Athens and Suda Bay detachments have not yet arrived but will probably do so within a few days. Will take the replacement machine at once and have wired Cologne to despatch the first two machines (of 216 Squadron). 214 Squadron have done very well and am hoping that 216 Squadron will be through by the end of the month.

But three days later he was in trouble with the now largely theoretical flying boat escort. McLaren contacted the Air Ministry:

> Pilots of the F3 (flying boats) at Alexandria have been returned to Malta. There is only one second pilot left at Alex. and he is on the sick list. Please advise me where I can obtain pilots. Very urgent.

In July the Air Ministry began collecting pilots, back in England, for the twenty-four extra machines that it was now planned to send in addition to the three squadrons at first intended. This doubled the number of machines involved.

> Director of Training and Organisation to Director of Personnel.
>
> Please arrange for 8 HP pilots of 274 Squadron at Bircham Newton to be posted to No.1 Aerial Route.

When reading the correspondence and deciphering the telegrams, which were mostly corrupted in transmission, one gets the impression that, because of the crisis in the Middle East, the Aerial Route staff were being stampeded into pushing the planes along without being given the necessary logistical support. Government-imposed cuts in expenditure must have been at the heart of the problem. This was the first time that any Air Force anywhere had tried to fly so many planes over such a long distance. McLaren was becoming discontented with the lack of support from the Navy, the Air Ministry and the AOC Middle East. On 31 July he requested an interview in London with Brigadier Game, the Director of Training and Organization. He didn't get this interview until he was relieved of his duties on 21 November, by which time there was little more to do than tidying up, closing down and writing off the machines that were never going to finish the course.

Another machine (F304) of 216 Squadron, with 1st Pilot Lieutenant Collinge, 2nd Pilot Lieutenant Adams, Rigger Aspley and Engine Fitter Balfour, made forced landings near Rouen and again near Avignon, caused by dirty petrol clogging the carburettors.

After further repairs the HP lifted off to continue on its way to the aerodrome at Istres near Marseille. This airfield was a barren, arid place, dust dry in the hot sun. Collinge jumped down after landing and, taking his .45 service revolver, shot a large scorpion. Each of the crew had been issued with a side arm in case the machine made a forced landing along the coast of North Africa where the native Senussi tribesmen were hostile because they were in the pay of the Turks. Orders then were to destroy the aircraft and then shoot oneself before unspeakable things were perpetrated by the locals. Unsurprisingly, the crews chose the northern Mediterranean route (via Crete) rather than the African one (via Malta).[1]

The sandbank at the mouth of the River Paillon just west of Nice and at the extreme end of the Promenade des Anglais. This is where Collinge landed. (Air1/2689/15/312/126)

F304 had another forced landing on the Promenade des Anglais at Nice and a waiter arrived with a tray of fruit for the crew, with the compliments of a nearby hotel manager.[2] The plane was repaired and, because it had folding wings, was moved by road to the airfield near Fréjus.

The local newspaper *L'Eclaireur de Nice* carried a full report of the graceful arrival of the Handley Page on the sandbank at the mouth of the River Paillon just west of the city, which was already called 'California' and designated as the city's future airport. With safety in mind, the newspaper also reminded local farmers that allowing their horses and cattle to graze on the airfield was absolutely forbidden.

From Fréjus they took off on the oversea leg over the Gulf of Genoa, making for Pisa. One engine ran out of oil and seized and they found that the plane was unable to maintain height on one engine alone. They were not far from the mountainous Italian coast and Collinge did his best to maintain a shallow glide towards it but just failed to reach the shoreline. The machine came down in a gentle glide on to the sea and Collinge, concentrating on the landing, forgot to undo his safety harness. As the wheels and undercarriage hit the water the machine tipped up on its nose. The other three members of the crew jumped clear but

127

The view of Cannes in 1919 just before turning south to cross the Bay of Genoa.
(Air 1/2689/15/312/126)

Collinge went underwater with the cockpit. By the time the others had realized his plight it was too late. He was dead when they finally managed to extricate him. An Italian coast guard launch soon arrived and took the three survivors and the body into Monterosso al Mare, about ten miles north of Spezia. This was the very accident that Borton had thought possible when he flew across the Bay of Genoa the previous year.

The Handley Page remained afloat in calm water and was towed into Spezia by the Italian Navy. Collinge was buried next day in the village cemetery just outside Monterosso. It is a striking site, which covers the whole of the top of a 'sugar loaf' hill overlooking the sea and the town of Monterosso. I drove there in vain in 2001 to photograph his grave, not knowing that in 1974 his remains had been transferred to the large British war cemetery at Ravenna where they could be maintained more easily at British expense. See the photo of the Monterosso cemetery in the colour section.

The day that Collinge shot the scorpion at Istres was his twenty-first birthday. He came from Larkfield in Kent and was an old boy of Maidstone Grammar School.[3]

Despite this experience, the 2nd Pilot, Adams, a Canadian, and the mechanic, Aspley, were detailed to take a second plane,

128

The cemetery outside Ravenna to which Collinge's remains were moved in 1974 so that the grave could be tended more easily. He is surrounded by Eighth Army men who fought their way up Italy and died in the closing weeks of World War Two. (CS)

Collinge's final grave at Ravenna. (CS)

D5445, from Marquise, near Calais, to Egypt in late August. They followed the Loire to Lyon and then flew over the Alps to Pisa and Taranto, navigating all the while with a picture post card map. They had a heavy landing at Taranto, which damaged the undercarriage, but managed to fly on again towards Albania where they had yet another forced landing on the beach near Valona. One engine had a cracked water jacket and was over-heating. They refilled the jacket with water from a stream, filtered through Tom Aspley's service cap and then just managed to take off, using the whole of the available beach. They landed at Athens as intended. The machine was firmly picketed for the night but was nevertheless blown away and completely destroyed. The crew completed the journey by train to Constantinople and then to Kantara in Egypt where 216 Squadron was based. They did not get there until early in 1920.

Yet another machine of 216 (C9714) had petrol trouble and made a forced landing on the beach at Albenga within days of the drowning of Lieutenant Collinge. The trouble was remedied and the pilot, Lieutenant Coke-Gee, tried to take off again but got stuck in soft sand. The nose pitched over into a deep pool of water with an incoming tide. Everybody got out except Coke-Gee who, like poor Collinge, was trapped underwater by the control wheel (joystick) but with one arm visible. An Italian motorist was a witness and immediately stripped off his jacket and dived in. He managed to wrench Coke-Gee sufficiently free to be able to hold his head above water until more help came. The motorist was recommended for a tangible reward of some kind but the Air Ministry file does not relate whether he got it. His name is given as 'Policisto Vittorio', which suggests that he was a policeman and that only his first name was recorded. He undoubtedly saved Coke-Gee's life.[4]

Coke-Gee's wounds went septic and he was in hospital for a month. Another machine, D8811, was allotted to him at St Raphael on 28 August and he spent the next two days working on the engines, only to have the machine wrecked by a storm the next night. He was allocated yet another machine on 30 September which, it seems, reached Cairo safely.

Meanwhile, the party of additional personnel to man the route stations, of which my father was one, had been assembled at RAF Halton.

RAF officers on His Majesty's Transport *Huntsman* as she was leaving Taranto. (LGS)

The journey overland to Taranto was 1,500 miles and took seven days. Some nights they slept on the train but at Faenza after the Alps they had a night in a specially provided rest house and had time for some sightseeing.

Disembarking at Salonika. (LGS)

131

The fitters and riggers destined for the route station at Suda. From left to right: Briggs, Perkins, Dale, Capper and Westbrook. The photo was taken while HMT *Huntsman* was in dock at Salonika. Captain Lewis is the shorter officer on the left. (LGS)

At Taranto there was a large mess full of British and Australian officers, travelling in both directions since this was the junction of the land and sea routes between Britain and Egypt. The mess was full so they slept in the train again. They embarked from Taranto on 9 July on the troopship HMT *Huntsman* and reached Constantinople on 24 July having first disembarked some officers

Men outside a mosque in Constantinople. They are washing their feet before going into the mosque as they still do today. (LGS)

Boats in the harbour at Constantinople. (LGS)

Arriving at Suda. Left centre can be seen the barracks that the Royal Navy built in 1897. The white, round topped blob between the two moored boats is the seaplane hangar. (Q14028)

and men at Salonika where there was still a garrison that included two RAF squadrons.

On 25 July, Major McLaren, still in charge of No. 1 Aerial Route, reported on the condition of the Suda Bay airfield. He reported it as perfectly level with a good surface but noted that it would need drainage for winter use (which it did not get). He also pointed out that the mountains on Crete that had to be crossed if machines flew direct to Africa were 5,000 feet high and not 8,000 as had been supposed in London. This was because planes could fly between Mount Ida and the White Mountains, across the Askifou plateau and out into the Mediterranean above the Imbros Gorge. This route was further west and shorter than the one that Borton had used.

Philby and Lawrence who had been delayed by problems with spares at Suda Bay, but were now safely in Cairo, had the ear of Major General Geoffrey Salmond. He complained to the Air Ministry in London. Major McLaren came under attack at St Raphael and he in turn criticized the staff at the Route Stations. In the correspondence file there is a letter to Major McLaren from Captain Lewis, written at Taranto on about 12 July, pointing out that he and Semple have not yet reached Suda Bay so that it can hardly be their fault if the service at Suda Bay is unsatisfactory. Lewis says in his letter that they had expected to do the train journey across France and Italy on the Rapide express but were obliged to use a slow troop train instead. They had money problems to sort out because the men travelling with them should have been given three weeks' wages in advance before they left RAF Halton and this had not been done. Nor had the men been issued with tropical kit. Lewis said that they expected to reach Suda Bay by 19 July. In fact, they only left Taranto on that date and took a further five days to reach Constantinople.[5]

Notes

1. T.J. Aspley & Peter Wright, 'Blazing the Trail', *Cross & Cockade*, Vol. 20 No. 2.
2. This is a charming story, taken from one second-hand version of the news, but doesn't accord with the account in the local paper.
3. Charles Ingham Collinge. Larkfield, Kent. Born 24.7.1898.
4. Air 1/2054/204/410/4.
5. Air 1/2054/204/410/3.

CHAPTER 12

'It Has Been a Complete Failure'

The next page of my father's photograph album is headed 'Suda Bay Crete August 2 to 27 December'. If the Admiralty had kept to its plans, Lewis and Semple would have arrived there two days after the Royal Navy abandoned the seaplane base. There are several photos of the naval air station, which was inside the former Turkish military Arsenal with a protective wall around it. There are also photographs of European girls who are certainly not Greek or Turkish looking. There was a primitive British military hospital on the island so perhaps they were Australian or British nurses. We know that they looked after several pilots who went down with sandfly fever, but from the photographs, they seem to have spent their spare time playing tennis.

The transport situation improved soon after Lewis and Semple arrived. In place of the old Ford T truck in the photograph of Borton's plane at Suda, there was now a smart open-topped Ford Tourer available for their use. This would have been just what twenty-year-old Semple needed to cut a dash with the nurses. He photographed it several times in and around Chania. He also seems to have taken aerial photos of Suda Bay and Chania from the cockpit of a Handley Page but they are uncaptioned.

Lewis and Semple should have been pleased with their accommodation when they disembarked at Manolis pier, Suda Bay on 2 August. They had use of the former British Admiral's house with its garden overlooking the bay and plenty of trees for shade.

The view of Suda Bay from the well-shaded garden of the Admiral's house. (LGS)

Lewis and Semple may have had comfortable accommodation in the Admiral's house but all was not well. Money problems continued. On 1 June responsibility for both the seaplane and the landplane bases at Suda Bay had been transferred from the GOC Aegean at Constantinople to the GOC Mediterranean at Malta.

The officers' mess at Suda. It had been the British Admiral's house during the Protectorate. Note the horse-drawn carriage in the shade on the right of the photo. There were no cars apart from the government-supplied Ford and this carriage was the only taxi in the town of Suda. In it the journey from the seaplane base to the airfield took half an hour. (LGS)

A Handley Page O/400 over Crete in 1919. The photo must have been taken from the rear gunner's cockpit. The airstrip at Suda was the only practical landing place. A big enough plateau existed high in the mountains to the south but there was only a goat track to it. (LGS)

Captain Charles Lewis, OC RAF Suda.

Lieutenant Leslie Semple, 2IC RAF Suda. (LGS)

A view of Suda from the north taken from a Handley Page in 1919. The village is in the bottom left-hand corner with one of the jetties projecting into the bay. The photo was taken by my father. (LGS)

A view of Suda twenty-two years later. This time taken from the south and from the cockpit of a Stuka dive-bomber. The four jetties of the Protecting Admirals are still there but one has been greatly enlarged. (IWM Collection 8404-13)

But Malta had no drachmas so couldn't pay the men at Suda Bay. In a letter to the Director of Personnel at the Air Ministry on 17 August 1920, long after Lewis had left the Air Force, he explained what had happened to £54 in the airmen's mess savings account.

> The Director of Personnel,
> Air Ministry, 17 August 1920
> London.
>
> Sir,
>
> The rationing of the men at the seaplane base Suda Bay was not good. To augment this most of them had purchased many of their meals at a neighbouring cafe. As their pay was very much in arrears many of them apparently had accounts at this establishment. On receiving sudden orders for them to be sent away, I found that they had not nearly enough money to pay their accounts. I was most anxious that they should leave here without leaving any debts so I divided the Mess Savings account balance between them evenly and personally made sure that all the debts were paid.
>
> Receipts, signed in triplicate, were left behind for Major Brotherton, but, having no clerk (our complete establishment at the time was 2 officers, 3 fitters R.R. and 1 rigger), it is quite possible that these papers were mislaid.
>
> I may say that when I arrived in Suda Bay I found the men in a singularly destitute state, not having received any pay at all for two months and being as much as four months or more in arrears. If verification of these statements is required I have no doubt that Mr Semple (Late Lt. RAF) who was under me at Suda will confirm them.
>
> I have the honour to be,
> Sir,
> Your obedient servant,
> C.A. Lewis[1]

When Brigadier Borton had made his flight the previous summer, he had two destroyers lying in wait on his route in case of ditching. Now all that was available was one seaplane at Suda Bay and it was less reliable than the Handley Pages that it was theoretically going to escort.

On 3 August Squadron Leader Welsh, the commander of 214 Squadron, sent a stinging complaint to the Air Ministry, via his boss, Geoffrey Salmond, in Egypt, about the standard of service that his squadron had received along the route.[2]

> The assistance rendered by the Route Station officers at the majority of the stations was negligible. They appeared to know nothing of the route except the station which they commanded. They were not even able to give the course and the bearings for the next stage of the journey.
>
> Planes often arrived unexpectedly and waited hours before anyone with authority arrived. The one object of the route officers appeared to be to get the machines off their aerodrome as soon as possible, irrespective of their condition. No assistance was ever rendered by the mechanics at the Route Stations.
>
> It was impossible to get weather reports in time to be of use before the planes were due to take off. So they had to wait until the next day, by which time the forecasts were out of date. Doubts about the weather greatly increased the responsibility and the worry for the pilots.
>
> No rations or accommodation were provided at Suda and in some cases we had to wait for spares to come from Salonika. One flight of four planes flew unescorted from Taranto to Africa.

These criticisms were sent on to Captain Lewis at Suda, to which he replied:

> Again, these complaints date from before Semple and I arrived so the responsibility rests with the seaplane station. We have no meteorology station near here and no wireless. No spares arrived here until the end of August although the seaplane base indented for them in June. Escorts have never been at my disposal and have never been obtainable when we wired for them from Malta.

The comments of the Canadian pilots of the record-breaking HP F318, were added to the 214 Squadron commander's list of complaints:

> The Station Commander at Lyon was absent for five days so we refuelled ourselves. At Istres there were no British staff at all and the French had never even heard of No.1 Aerial Route. At Pisa the CO turned up hours after we had refuelled and overhauled our machines ourselves. At Rome the CO agreed to refuel while we had breakfast. The petrol arrived three hours later although the petrol store was only 100 yards away. Captain Horn expressed regret that no labour was available and then disappeared into Rome for the day and left us to refuel ourselves.

Refuelling a Handley Page. This shows refuelling the easy way. All too often, no pump was available and about sixty-five four-gallon jerry cans had to be manhandled from the ground to the tanks in the fuselage. Note the warning about keeping clear of revolving propellers. Several airmen in France were killed by these. (IWM Q 11534)

There were problems in getting the spares delivered all along the route. Vital components were sent by train but there were difficulties with stationmasters so couriers were sent with the spares instead. A petrol shipment disappeared en route. One staging post commander was absent looking for it at a critical moment and another was on leave, with permission, in Rome during what was thought to be a lull in the traffic. He was recalled but the telegram did not reach him in time. One machine (D8323) made a forced landing on the Greek coast at Amyro because it had run out of petrol. It was impossible to get petrol to it by lorry and so HMS *Swallow* was sent from Alexandria. By the time the petrol arrived the pilot had gone down with sandfly fever and had to be admitted to hospital. The pilot complained of difficulty in finding the Suda Bay airfield and when Lewis and Semple arrived at Suda they were requested to have a horse shoe of white painted stones laid out to make it easier to find. Presumably, the barrow loads of white chalk that the Navy had laid down the year before had lost their fresh white appearance. The machine and its crew finally reached Heliopolis on 28 July.

HP F305 had an eventful but pointless journey. It was damaged at Istres by the same mistral that damaged D5418. Its wings were repaired and it set off again but had a forced landing on a beach near San Remo on 8 August while flying across the Bay of Genoa. Some reduction gearing had been stripped and a new engine was needed. This was obtained and fitted on the beach.

After waiting some time for the mistral to abate, the machine took off again on 2 September. It came into land at Pisa, but when only 400 feet from the ground, the elevators jammed and the machine crashed on its nose on the airfield. No one was hurt but the machine was written off. The jamming was probably caused by rusting control wires, which failed to slip through their guiding pulleys. Hydraulic controls were still in the future.

The construction of the HP O/400 made the pilot and observer vulnerable when the machine crashed nose first – as most did. The petrol tanks, which held nearly three tons of petrol, were located at the centre of gravity of the aeroplane, which was not far behind the cockpit.

Its predecessor, the HP O/100, carried its petrol in the engine nacelles, out on the wings, which was a much safer place to store it. But this limited the amount of fuel carried to 100 gallons with

It is difficult to understand how anyone survived these nose first crashes. The cockpits of the gunner, the pilot and the observer have completely disappeared, crushed by the weight of the petrol tanks. Yet in this crash no one was seriously injured. (LGS)

each engine. The O/400 could carry 300 gallons and this increased its range. Safety took second place to efficiency.

Another gale casualty on No. 1 Route was HP C9743 – a former 207 Squadron machine. This had repeated engine trouble on the

The front half of the skeleton of an HP O/400. The position of the petrol tanks in relation to the pilot and observer's cockpit is all too evident. (HP 818)

143

journey, probably due to particles of perished rubber from the feed pipes to the carburettors getting into the petrol. When it reached St Raphael both engines were removed for overhaul or replacement. The real problem with the petrol feed pipes had not yet been identified. It only arose with planes that had been exposed to the sun for some time. Borton, in a brand-new machine, had no problems. C9743 was securely moored but the wind got up on 9 August. Without engines, the wind ripped it from its moorings and wrecked it.

Despite the mishaps, the Air Ministry decided that the aerial route should be secured for the longer term. Negotiations began to purchase the Suda Bay airfield and build an aerodrome big enough to house eight machines, sixteen officers and twenty-four other ranks. The seaplane base was also to be kept open for five machines, ten officers and fifteen other ranks and accommodation for both groups of people would be pooled. Negotiations were entrusted to a bright young diplomat called Harold Nicolson who had got to know Prime Minister Venizelos during the Paris Peace Conference.

Mr Venizelos pointed out, in the nicest possible way, for he was a charming man, that the British couldn't assume that they could establish military bases on other people's territory now that the war was over. If the Greeks granted Britain sovereignty over a base on Crete, the Italians would want one on the Dodecanese Islands. Instead it was agreed that the Greeks would build the airbase and retain sovereignty but allow the British to use it in return for the gift of 100 aeroplanes, flying instructors and guidance on the development of a Greek Air Force. This seemed a good idea to the Air Ministry because they were anxious to establish influence over Greek aviation development for the sake of the British aircraft industry. There was already strong competition from the French but in long-distance, load-carrying machines, Britain led the world.[3] This leadership did not last much longer.

On 16 August 1918 the Air Ministry notified McLaren that it was intended to send six Vickers Vimys to Egypt as well as the HPs. This was the first occasion on which Vimys were brought into service in the RAF, although one had been used for Alcock and Brown's transatlantic flight. Its name was no doubt chosen because that flight was its baptism and the flight began in Canada.

It was the Canadians who had so distinguished themselves in the battle for Vimy Ridge, Arras, in April 1917

Completion of the transfer of planes to Egypt was given an added urgency because at this stage the Italians had not changed their minds about closing the accommodation for British mechanics at Italian airfields, although they had granted an extension until 15 October.

HP B8813, one of the replacement machines, never even started the journey before it was wrecked. A gale blew up at Buc, outside Paris, on 17 August and while the machine was being hurriedly wheeled into a hangar, the tail was blown off the skid trolley and the fuselage was cracked by the fall to the ground.

McLaren wrote to the Air Ministry on 18 August:

> Essential that machines delivered to me should be in better condition. Four machines are now scattered over the route with broken reduction gears. Impossible to cope with all this with present personnel. Delays inevitable unless better machines delivered.

The persistent trouble with stripped reduction gears was later attributed to poor quality ball bearings, which had been supplied from the USA.

McLaren to OC Suda Bay – Captain Lewis on 19 August:

> Lewis and Semple will not be required to fly machines to Matruh but will remain as ground officers. Semple is surplus to requirements but will stay as your sickness cover because of difficulty in making replacements. One F3 (flying boat) is to be under your command at Suda, supplied by GOC Mediterranean. Machines will arrive at Suda in flights of four. They are to fly direct to Matruh only stopping at Sollum if fuel is running low because of headwinds.

My father's scrap book contains an envelope that was used for carrying official mail from the Headquarters of No. 1 Aerial Route at St Raphael near Marseilles to 'I' Route Station at Suda Bay, Crete. The envelope makes it clear that the route from France to Cairo was No. 1 Aerial Route and not the route from Cairo to India as most RAF historians suggest. See colour photo. Most communication was by telegraph since no long-distance telephone lines existed. This letter went by airmail. Providing the aeroplane did not crash en route, this was preferable to telegraph because telegrams were usually badly corrupted (see below).

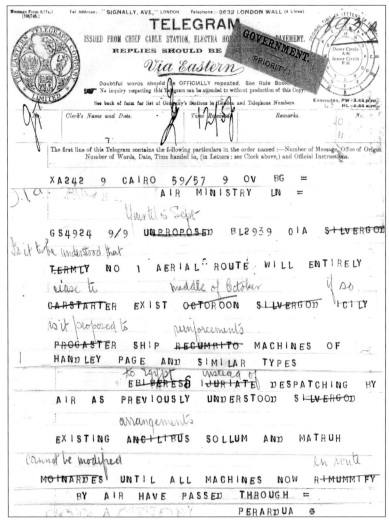

The telegram from GHQ Cairo seeking clarification of the decision to close No. 1 Aerial Route. The telegram was probably sent in cipher, which may have added to the difficulties. How and when the pencilled corrections were made is not known. There were no telephones or wireless over these distances. Long-distance wireless transmission from the post office radio station at Rugby was still five years away. (Air 2/107/A17762)

HP C9716 crashed on 2 September, the same day as HP F305. It was another of the former 207 Squadron machines and encountered the same petrol trouble as did all the others, including the three that did not crash (see the Court of Enquiry findings). It made a crash-landing in a vineyard near Albenga on the Italian Riviera. In Major McLaren's opinion it was the pilot's fault. 'He could undoubtedly have chosen a more suitable landing ground.' It is a characteristic of the English language that when somebody uses the word 'undoubtedly' the one thing that is certain is that the matter is in doubt. No one was hurt.

HP D5445 left Buc on 29 July. It had a chequered flight and was fitted with a new radiator, new petrol tanks and new controls at Istres. It left Istres on 2 September but for some reason did not leave Taranto until 21 September. This was the plane in which Adams and Aspley were travelling, survivors of the fatal crash in the sea near Monterosso. They were then forced to land for petrol at Valona in Albania because of strong headwinds. During the night a gale blew up and the plane was blown from its moorings. A sister machine, F316, also at Valona, was blown on to the top of the petrol shed.

HP J2246 had five forced landings while it was crossing France, all caused by petrol trouble. It left Entrecaisteaux near Draguignan on 30 September on the final leg of the journey over France but the pilot got lost and came down in the sea at St Aygulf near St Raphael. The crew was rescued, but not the machine.

On 8 September news came through from the British Embassy in Rome that the Italians had agreed to an extension of facilities until 30 November, in return for similar facilities for them at Heliopolis. This made a more realistic timetable possible.

Now we come to perhaps the most notable tragedy.

> Air Attaché, British Embassy Rome to Air Ministry Sept. 29th.
>
> Vickers Vimy 8622 crashed near Bracciano and caught fire. Captain C.H. Darley killed. Captain C.O. Darley burned but will recover. Funeral of Captain Darley in Rome tomorrow.

The full details of what had happened were given in a private letter from Major McLaren to his boss Brigadier Game, at the Air Ministry. The Vickers Vimy had left Pisa late and the pilot realized that he would not reach Rome in daylight because of headwinds. He made a straightforward landing in a field close to the seaplane base at Capua on Lake Bracciano, thirty miles north of Rome. The crew included C.H. Darley's brother as observer and Captain Hudson, the OC of the Pisa Aerial Route Station, as passenger. They spent the night at the seaplane base.

The next morning they got ready to take off but at the last minute Captain Hudson, who was reconnoitring alternative landing grounds for Major McLaren, decided to get out of the plane because of some change of plan. Reading between the lines, there may have been a disagreement between Hudson and Darley. Hudson stood and watched the take-off. Captain Darley, perhaps in a bad mood, put the plane to full throttle and roared away but failed to notice a pair of telegraph poles and the wires between them at the edge of the field. Too late he veered to the right, but his left wing hit one of the poles and the machine swung round and crashed in flames. The mechanic and Captain C.O. Darley, the observer, were thrown clear but Captain C.H. Darley was trapped beneath the petrol tanks. Captain C.O. Darley ran back into the flames to try to rescue his brother. He failed and retreated, badly burned and blinded.

Captain Darley's grave in the St Paolo cemetery at Rome. It is beside those of Lieutenants Prince and Spratt who were killed at Centocelle. Darley appears to have been given a posthumous promotion, perhaps for the sake of his wife's pension. (CS)

Captain Darley, who was thirty, was an experienced pilot. He had been flying Handley Pages since they first went into service in 1917 and had been awarded the DSC for carrying out bombing missions on Bruges where the Germans had a large submarine base. He came from Edgbaston but his next of kin, either his wife or his mother, was living in Kensington when he died.[4]

Apparently, pilots were still leaving Pisa late for what seemed the relatively short hop to Rome. They had not been allowing for a frequently encountered headwind so that they approached Rome as it was getting dark. A stern instruction was now issued to leave Pisa before 1 p.m. in future. No doubt crews had been indulging in a bit of sightseeing in the mornings. Foreign travel was still a novelty and for many it was a chance to sample the eighteenth century gentleman's 'grand tour' at government expense. The situation was not helped by the very poor accommodation offered to the officers at Pisa and elsewhere. The result was that they declined it and went to a hotel in the town instead. This added to the temptation to go sightseeing and, incidentally, made it more difficult for those who came after them, because, lacking any

There was plenty of sightseeing to do. With no air traffic control to worry about one could approach Centocelle by flying over St Peter's. This photograph was taken by McLaren in December 1918 from his four-engined Handley Page.
(Air 1/2689/15/312/126)

foreign allowance from the RAF before they set off, they simply presented cheques that bounced.

This view of events is confirmed by the recollections of Air Mechanic George West of 216 Squadron. He left Marquise near Calais on 10 July 1919 in Handley Page J2256, piloted by Flight Lieutenant Jaques but did not reach Cairo until 14 September. Progress was slow, with various mechanical troubles, accidental damage and bad weather. West also thought that the rather generous expenses allowed to these particular officers caused not a little delay in flying the route, which was by this time strewn with HP wrecks. They changed propellers at Suda but the replacements, which were cannibalized, as before, from Liberty flying boats, had brass tips and were twelve inches smaller in diameter. This meant that they could not fly higher than 2,000 feet and had to fly round the west end of the island to avoid the mountains. When they arrived in Cairo the machine was so battered that the engines were removed and the rest was burnt.[5]

Similar criticisms came from Sergeant T.J. Aspley, whose crash in F304 with Lieutenant Collinge has already been described. They set off on that fatal flight from Marquise and reached Paris (Le Bourget) after a forced landing near Rouen.

Here the crew met up with the other Squadron members who had landed earlier. It seems as though there was no particular hurry to move on and some days and nights were spent in Paris seeing the sights. Some of the crews had not long before been engaged in the deadly serious business of wartime operations with long hazardous flights over enemy territory. Perhaps they felt that the odd wild fling was only their due. The opportunities presented by the current journey were too good to miss so they enjoyed some high life.[6]

These criticisms of officers wasting time enjoying themselves did not, however, apply to Captain Darley and his crew. Captain Darley was a serious and experienced pilot and they were late on their flight because they were attempting to do the two stages from Istres to Pisa and from Pisa to Rome in one day.

The crash caused a stir in England when news of it appeared in the papers. Captain Darley was well known as the pilot of one of the four-engined Handley Page V1500s that was on the runway waiting to take-off to bomb Berlin when the Armistice was signed. Instead he made the first flight from London to Madrid in a similar machine. He had a forced landing on the beach at Biarritz on the way out but reached Madrid safely and was feted. He had another forced landing near Biarritz on the way back but this time the machine veered into the sea and broke up. The crew were rescued by fishermen, just in time to escape a rising tide. Despite this failure, they were again feted and put up in the *Palace Hotel*. They slept the night in the royal suite where Asquith had kissed hands with Edward VII on his appointment as Prime Minister in 1908.[7]

Darley had survived an even earlier crash in France on the night of 11 December 1917. He had hit trees coming in to land in his Handley Page. The machine was completely wrecked and Darley ended up with his head trapped for more than an hour underneath one of the engines with petrol pouring over him. But on that occasion the machine had not caught fire and he was flying again two days later. His co-pilot that night had been Captain Gilmour who was now the OC of Route Station E at Rome and therefore expected to see his old friend when he landed at Capua that day.

The Lake Bracciano tragedy, coming on top of all the other bad news, greatly depressed McLaren and he had a poor opinion of many of the officers who had been assigned to the Aerial Route. In a private letter to his boss, Brigadier Game, following Darley's death he wrote:

> All this is very disheartening and discouraging as I have put my heart and soul into making a good show of No. 1 Aerial Route and now I cannot but admit that it has been a complete failure. I am aware of the adage 'a bad workman always complains of his tools' but some of these officers who have passed through and some of those who are under my command are about as much use as a sick cat when it comes to doing a job of work.[8]

The next casualty on the route was HP B8811, another 207 Squadron machine. Like the others, this machine had petrol trouble all the way and eventually made a forced landing in a river bed at Hyères on 25 August. Somehow it got off again and reached St Raphael on 1 September where it was promptly

Captain Darley's crash on 11 December 1917. (Chaz Bowyer)

wrecked in a gale. This was Coke-Gee's second crash. He had nearly drowned in HP C9714 at St Raphael earlier in the summer.

At the end of September the position of planes on No. 1 Aerial Route was something like this:

58 Squadron 10 machines safely in Egypt.
D5434 crashed at Chalon. Written off.
D5439 crashed at Rome. Written off 17 May.

214 Squadron 5 machines in Egypt.
D8317 at St Raphael awaiting a replacement wing.
D4591 crashed at Treto. Written off 10 July.
C9743 destroyed in gale at St. Raphael. Written off 30 August.
J2257 at Pisa.

216 Squadron 6 machines in Egypt.
C9744 at Athens.
D5445 crashed at Valona. Written off 21 September.
D8811 at St Raphael.
J2246 forced landing at Aix en Provence and later crash-landed in sea off St Raphael where it slowly sank into the sand and was written off on 30 September.

D5418 wrecked in gale at Istres. Written off 16 July.
F304 crashed into sea at Spezia. Written off 26 July.
F305 Damaged in gale at Istres. Wings replaced. Crash-landed at Pisa. Written off 2 September.

Replacements D5429 at Athens.
F316 crashed at Valona. Written off 21 September.
B8813 crashed at Buc. Written off 17 August.
C9714 crashed at Albenga. Written off 3 September.
D4596 at Taranto.
J2256 at Pierrelatte.
D5429 at Lyon.

Vickers Vimys 8614 at St Raphael.
8615, 8616, 8617, at Buc (Paris).
8622 crashed at Bracciano. Written off 28 September.

So, at this stage twenty-nine machines were either in Egypt or more or less airworthy en route and thirteen had been written off. That still left nine machines dotted about, of doubtful airworthiness. Winter was approaching and the Air Ministry was getting worried.

The following telegram was sent by the Air Ministry to No. 1 Aerial Route St Raphael on 28 October.

> Inform me if Suda Bay airfield is yet under water. If not when? No risk is to be run with machines. Is it possible for machines to be moved by ship from Suda Bay to Egypt?

On 7 November a reply to this telegram came direct from Suda Bay to the Air Ministry:

> Suda Bay aerodrome is at present in good condition. Should last until November 20 but cannot give certain info. Impossible transfer machines by Greek ferry Egypt but could put them on suitable English ship if sent.

The reply came direct from Suda Bay via the telegraph office in Chania because Major McLaren was at that moment moving his HQ forward from St Raphael near Marseille to Taranto on the

153

heel of Italy. All the remaining airworthy machines had reached Taranto by then and Major McLaren realized, perhaps a little late in the day, that Taranto was better positioned for control of the most difficult part of the route. The most important element in this message from Captain Lewis is that it *was* possible to send Handley Pages by sea whereas some people had said at the outset of the project that this was not feasible. It was possible because the machines had folding wings, which were therefore detachable. Engines were routinely removed for maintenance so a machine naturally separated into five components – two wings, two engines and an admittedly long fuselage.

There is a distinct change of tone in the telegram sent by the Air Ministry to McLaren on 28 October. Now the emphasis has changed from pushing the machines on regardless, to 'no risk is to be run'. There was good reason for this change. News of the high death toll and the loss of machines on the London to Cairo route was in all the papers and the Secretary of State for Air, Winston Churchill, had ordered an enquiry. It was the following news-paper cutting, which I found in my father's scrapbook, that led me to research and write this book.

A Handley Page O/400 with its wings folded. (IWM Q12105)

LONDON – CAIRO AIR DEATHS
11 LIVES LOST

The Daily Mail is informed that in the last few months 11 airmen flying Air Ministry machines to Egypt have lost their lives through failure of their engines over the Mediterranean or through crashing when landing on unsuitable aerodromes. The Air Ministry Commission, it is understood, is to investigate the condition of the machines at starting, and whether adequate arrangements were made at the refuelling points.

One of the airmen killed is Captain C.H. Darley, D.S.C., D.F.C. who early this year made a flight to Madrid in a four engined Handley Page machine. Captain Darley, it is understood, was killed on September 29th at Bracciano near Rome, when his Vickers Vimy twin engined machine crashed and caught fire.

On his return from a flight to Nice Col. G.L.P. Henderson, M.C., A.F.C. until lately in charge of the Avro passenger flying at Hounslow, told the London Evening News that he had given his solemn promise to officers stranded along the route to get the present state of affairs remedied.

30 PER CENT FAILURES

'Three squadrons of Handley Page machines' said Col. Henderson 'were ordered to proceed from their depots in France to Egypt. I understand that 30 per cent of them failed to reach their destinations. To my knowledge 11 airmen were killed, including Captain Darley. Cases were brought to my notice of officers and airmen stranded in Italy for weeks without any pay.

One Handley Page with two pilots fell into the water. One pilot was rescued by the Italians, the other was drowned. The rescued man was immediately sent back for another machine, and it was on his second attempt that I found him "down" with troubles of all sorts, doing his utmost to repair his machine. It is not the fault of the machines or the pilots. There was complete lack of competent riggers and mechanics.

There is no organisation and after leaving Marseilles the conditions are appalling.

There is a 250 mile flight across water to be made and at present there is no machine that could be run on that route by any commercial firm with a hope of making it a success. No business concern would ever attempt to transport machines to Egypt by air. It would be far cheaper to pack them and send them by water.

£110,000 ACCIDENTS[9]

Between Marseilles and Nice I came across wrecked Handley Pages, or rather what was left of them. Quite apart from the irreparable loss of these gallant fellows I have spoken of, the accidents represent a sum of £110,000. I asked a lot of fellows whom I came across, stranded on what the Air Ministry calls "The Blazing Trail", the cause of their troubles. In nearly every case it was the same. Rubber connections of various parts of the engines had perished and other parts were in a deplorable condition; and there was no expert assistance within hundreds of miles.

I want to make clear that I do not think that responsibility rests with the military of the R.A.F. who I know are engaged on very excellent work.'

FULLEST ENQUIRY
STATEMENT BY GENERAL SEELY
UNDER-SECRETARY FOR AIR

Sir W. Joynson Hicks, in the House of Commons, asked the Under Secretary for Air whether his attention had been called to statements recently made by Col. Henderson as to the number of deaths of pilots on the air route to Egypt.

General Seely said that in the early summer the Secretary to the War Office sent the Air Ministry an urgent call for Handley Page machines to meet a situation that was then described as critical. At the end of April there was an urgent telegraphic request for additional squadrons, and, in view of the fact that no Handley Page machines had been packed and sent by sea, it was decided that the machines must be sent by air to meet the emergency although considerable risk was necessarily involved.

At the end of April the first squadron was ordered to proceed and it left on May 3rd. Special arrangements were made by sending out an officer of practical knowledge to arrange facilities, for landing, the supply of spares, petrol etc. On account of the accidents which occurred an officer was then stationed at each aerodrome en route to assist the aviators in every possible way. Great difficulties were however experienced by the officers not being able to get telephone or telegraphic messages through in time for action to be taken and the inability to get the necessary spares to the points required owing to difficulties of transport.

It was also not found possible, owing to demobilisation, to get the best qualified personnel within the time available.

At present 51 Handley Page machines had left for Egypt. Of these 26 had arrived; 10 were on the later stages of the journey; and 15 had been written off as broken up or lost at sea. He emphasised that the making of this route had nothing to do with civil aviation.

The fullest enquiry would be made by the Committee already sitting, and, if it was found that mistakes had been made by anyone concerned from himself downwards he need hardly say appropriate action would be taken.

This politician's prose manages to obscure the fact that it had consciously been decided to fly the Handley Pages rather than ship them just as it obscures the fact that no thought had been given to retaining skilled mechanics in the squadrons concerned until the flights had been made. A bonus to the key men needed would probably have achieved this. The fact that the number of people required to man the route was seriously under estimated is also sidestepped.

It is not possible to reconcile Henderson's statement that eleven aircrew had been killed with the facts. The count in the Air Ministry files of the time only shows eight and that was confirmed in the Enquiry report. The account of the pilot who was obliged to press on in another plane immediately after a crash in which his co-pilot was drowned must refer to the accident to F304 of 216 Squadron off Spezia on 25 July.

> I want to make it clear that I do not think that responsibility rests with the military of the R.A.F. who I know are engaged on very excellent work.

Coming after what Colonel Henderson had already said, this statement is difficult to understand. One explanation might be that he blamed the Government, not the RAF, for failing to match expenditure to commitments – a situation which is not unknown today – and for forcing manpower cuts, which cost the RAF its most experienced mechanics.

General Seely's statement to Parliament that the decision to fly the machines to Cairo had nothing to do with the future development of civil aviation is obviously untrue. Brigadier Borton had used future air route planning as a main reason for undertaking his flight, as well as reinforcing the Air Force in Egypt and Palestine. Major General Sykes' paper on the future air power requirements of the Empire, published on 12 September 1918, also showed that it was air supremacy after the war that was in mind. Last but not least, Brigadier Groves had referred to 'the desirability, on the grounds of policy, of inaugurating this route as a step towards the development of aerial transport after the war.'

On 30 October General Game, the Director of Training and Organization at the Air Ministry, wrote to Major McLaren:

> I am directed to inform you that your presence is required at a Court of Enquiry being held at the Air Ministry and in order to enable your return arrangements have been made for Squadron Leader A.M. Wilson to take over your command.

McLaren appeared to be in trouble. He had been relieved of his command and ordered to attend a Court of Enquiry.

On 7 November McLaren told the Air Ministry that there were still seven machines along the route, plus one recently wrecked by gales at Athens, but he expected all the machines to be off the route by 20 November. The next day he sent closing down instructions to all the stations along the route except Suda Bay where both officers were ordered to remain until the last machine was through. On 13 November McLaren left Taranto for St Raphael, London, and the Court of Enquiry.

On the 15th the Air Ministry instructed the GOC Middle East not to dispense with the flying boat escort at Suda because there were still five machines to come. At this point the flying boat pilots, who were apparently NCOs, declined to make long flights unless they were granted temporary commissions. In fact, none of them had made any flights since July and the weather was now deteriorating. The file does not relate whether they won their point. They were perhaps overdue for demobilization and did not see why they should take the risk of flying backwards and forwards over the Mediterranean with less reward than the pilots they were escorting.

The Air Ministry sent another memo forbidding machines to fly the Mediterranean without an escort, but this was just to guard their backs. It had been going on all through the summer and Salmond in Cairo, and the AOC Mediterranean at Malta who was responsible for supplying the flying boats, must have known it. It was fortunate that there were no fatalities on the Suda Bay to Mersah Matruh (or Sollum) leg of the journey.

In an attempt to follow the Air Ministry instructions, a flying boat was sent from Alexandria to escort the last of the machines flying from Crete to Sollum but it was wrecked on the Greek coast and, once again, the bits were brought into Suda on a trawler.

With the enquiry now sitting, all RAF eyes were on No. 1 Aerial Route. Everyone was trying to cover his position.

Air Marshal Trenchard wrote to Air Officer Commanding Mediterranean on 29 November 1919:

> It is essential that we get the last four machines through safely and quickly from Suda Bay to Egypt and I look to you to do all you can to help.

And the Air Ministry was trying to pick up the pieces.

> Telegram Air Ministry to Taranto. 27th November.

> Collect up all the remaining machines at Suda Bay to await escort over Mediterranean. Ensure airfield at Suda Bay is still serviceable before sending machines on.

Telegram Taranto to Air Ministry London. 30th November.

Severe gales. D8317 wrecked and D5429 badly damaged. So only two serviceable machines remain. Not worth sending an escort for just two machines and Suda airfield now becoming risky. Suggest dismantle machines and ship parts by boat to Cairo.[10]

So now we have Major McLaren confirming what Captain Lewis had said earlier, namely that dismantling the machines and shipping the parts by boat to Cairo was perfectly feasible.

By this stage seventeen of the fifty-one aircraft involved on the first air route in the world had crashed or been destroyed and eight of the aircrew killed. Brigadier Game, the Director of Training and Organization, who had by this time abandoned his rank of Brigadier and assumed the RAF rank of Group Captain, agreed with the telegram from Taranto, and that was the end of No. 1 Aerial Route. It was officially stated that increased manufacturing facilities in Egypt made it redundant.

* * *

There are many Air Ministry files on the subject of No. 1 Aerial Route and about fifty photographs in The National Archive but the only published account that I have found is in Chaz Bowyer's meticulously detailed book – *Handley Page Bombers of the First World War*. His account of No. 1 Aerial Route takes only 1,500 words with three photographs but, as the title of his book implies, it is about the fate of the aircraft rather than the wisdom of the project or the views of the people involved. However he does say that the project 'was to prove a daunting test of the involved aircrews skills and endurance'. He describes McLaren's flight in the V/1500 and he also describes the crash of Lawrence's machine as it came in to land at Centocelle. But his only reference to the row that ensued between those who made the plans, those who flew, those who sent them, those who were supposed to look after them en route, and those who were supposed to pinpoint responsibility afterwards, was his use of the phrase 'When the dust had settled'.

He refers to the Cairo–Baghdad trail as the 'first stage' of the planned England to India route although there are many files in The National Archive that refer to 'No. 1 Aerial Route RAF' pioneered between England and Cairo in 1919 and I possess the official letter with its envelope stamped 'Headquarters of No. 1 Aerial Route, St Raphael, Marseilles', which was sent to my father when he succeeded to the command of the refuelling and servicing station at Suda Bay. See colour photo.

Responsibility for the RAF in France and Germany rested with Major General John Salmond who was the brother of Geoffrey, on the receiving end in Egypt. The only reference to No. 1 Aerial Route in the biography of John Salmond is as follows:

> Bombers from Britain and France were reconditioned and flown overland but several of them – Handley Pages mostly – crashed en route.[11]

John Salmond here makes the claim that the machines were re-conditioned before the journey but the subsequent enquiry made it clear that many of the machines were, in fact, in poor condition before they set off. John Salmond had ultimate responsibility for this. Too many skilled fitters had already been demobilized and the reconditioning was not as thorough as it should have been. No one seems to have learned for example that rubber tubes perish if exposed to strong sunlight and rubber was hardly a new invention.

Anne Baker, Geoffrey Salmond's daughter, has published a biography of her father. She describes in detail his part in pioneer-ing the air route from Cairo to India but omits any mention of the England to Cairo route for which he was the principal advocate.[12] It is difficult to forgive this because my own research shows that it is impossible to research the Cairo to India route in The National Archive (Public Record Office) without coming across the files relating to the ill-fated No. 1 Aerial Route to Cairo. One must conclude that she omitted any reference to it out of filial loyalty. It was the brainchild of her father and it was an abject failure.

There is no mention of No. 1 Aerial Route in Sir Frederick Sykes' biography but although he had authorized it, he had been out of the job of CAS for four months before the first plane took off.[13]

It is not mentioned in Trenchard's official biography but this is a special case. It was written by Lady Trenchard's grandson by her first marriage, Andrew Boyle, because no one else would agree to write it.[14] It is more of a eulogy than a biography. The close relationship between Trenchard and the writer is neither disclosed in the book nor even on the dust jacket. Boyle, at the age of seventeen, sat at Trenchard's death bedside taking notes.[15] The book was published six years later with Lady Trenchard's help. Boyle did lots of serious research but his bias is obvious. For one thing, he omitted Trenchard's vehement opposition to the formation of the RAF until it had become a *fait accompli*. Trenchard was not responsible for No. 1 Route's inception but he became Chief of the Air Staff at the moment that it was inaugurated and, despite his attack of influenza, was back in his office before the first plane set off from Paris.

Brigadier P.R.C. Groves was Director of Flying Operations at the Air Ministry when the decision to launch the Route was made. He supported it at the time and mentioned the pioneering flight to Egypt in his book *Behind the Smokescreen*, which was published in 1934. His authority evaporated when his boss Sykes was ousted as Chief of the Air Staff and he said no more about it in his book, which concentrated on the wider theme of the desperate need to build a much larger air force in face of the growing threat from Hitler.

Wing Commander Ian Philpott's book[16] begins with Trenchard's famous White Paper 'The Permanent Organisation of the RAF'. This White Paper was not published until December 1919 and his book thus avoids the controversy surrounding the collapse of No. 1 Aerial Route. This is ironic because the findings of the internal Air Ministry enquiry into the failure of that Route are direct pointers to some of the recommendations made in Trenchard's much applauded White Paper.

Roy Conyers Nesbit's book *The RAF, An Illustrated History From 1918* also overlooks the existence of No. 1 Aerial Route RAF between London and Cairo in 1919 despite its significance for the famous White Paper. The same is true of Air Chief Marshal Sir Michael Armitage's book published in 1993 *The Royal Air Force – An Illustrated History*.

Why historians of the RAF have 'overlooked' the fiasco of No. 1 Aerial Route is puzzling. Most of these writers are retired senior officers of the RAF but surely by now the reputation of the RAF is such that occasional mistakes in the past can be admitted without upsetting the *esprit de corps* of the Service. No. 1 Aerial Route was a failure but a lot was learnt from it that had a bearing on the future of the RAF. By comparison with other deliberate distortions of history this one is a mere trifle. For example, Charles de Gaulle managed to write a history of the French Army without mentioning the Battle of Waterloo.[17] What is remarkable about this RAF story is that *every* historian of the Service has side stepped it until now, apart from Chaz Bowyer in his very short edited account.

* * *

In due course it was agreed that the arrangements made between Harold Nicolson and Elutherios Venizelos for maintaining an RAF airfield at Suda Bay should be cancelled. The aerodrome at Suda was offered to the Greek government but the land still belonged to local Cretans who wanted £6,000 for it. The drainage alone was estimated at a further £30,000 and Greece decided that it had no use for it.[18]

Hearing this, the British Government asked that the land should not be built upon so that, in an emergency, the airfield could be brought back into use. This may explain why, to this day, some of the land is still used for market gardening whereas the expansion of the town of Chania has meant that most of its surroundings are covered with housing estates, motor car showrooms and supermarkets.

Notes

1. Incidentally, the author of this letter, Charles Lewis, is not to be confused with the better known Cecil Lewis, who had also been an RFC pilot. Cecil wrote *Sagittarius Rising* and was a founding father of the BBC. He settled in Corfu in later life whereas Charles Lewis settled in Chania and became secretary to the British Consul in Crete.
2. Air 1/2054/204/410/4.
3. Air 2/79/B1882, Air 2/80/B3425.
4. Cecil Hill Darley, 77 Fountain Road, Edgbaston, Birmingham. Born 11.3.1889.
5. *Cross & Cockade*, Vol. 12. No. 1 p. 28.
6. *Cross & Cockade*, Vol. 20. No. 2.
7. Air 1/1140/204/5/2312.
8. Air 2/126/B11479.
9. At least £11 million in today's money.

10. Air 2/107/A17762 Part 3.
11. John Laffin, *Swifter Than Eagles*. p.150. Blackwood 1964.
12. Anne Baker, *From Biplane to Spitfire*. Pen & Sword. 2003. She has also confused General McEwen with Major McLaren in recording Brigadier Borton's flight to Cairo.
13. Eric Ash – *Sir Frederick Sykes and the Air Revolution 1914–1918*. Frank Cass 1999.
14. T.E. Lawrence and Trenchard's ADC in France, Maurice Baring, both declined to write it.
15. Andrew Boyle – *Trenchard*. Collins. 1962.
16. Ian Philpott – *The Royal Air Force*, Volume 1, The Inter-War Years. Pen & Sword.
17. Charles de Gaulle, *La France et Son Armée*, 1938.
18. Air 2/79/B8044.

CHAPTER 13

The Court of Enquiry

News that there was to be a Court of Enquiry into what had gone wrong on No. 1 Aerial Route did not reach the newspapers until 1 November but Trenchard had, in fact, ordered it on 2 October, just three days after news of Captain Darley's crash reached London.[1]

CAS (Trenchard) to Under Secretary of State for Air (Seely):

> In view of the large number of crashes and forced landings which have occurred among HP and Vimy machines sent to Egypt along No. 1 Aerial Route, I should like to convene a Court of Enquiry to investigate the whole question of the inception of this route, its organisation and running.
>
> I should like the president and members to be officers who have had nothing whatever to do with the matter in any form and, so far as possible, those who have severed their direct connection with the RAF.
>
> I propose Air Vice Marshal Ellington as president and Air Commodore Brook-Popham, Group Captain Borton and Mr G.B. Cockburn as members.

Considering Trenchard's expressed desire to appoint an enquiry committee that was free of any involvement in the Route, his choice of Ellington as president and Borton as member was strange. Perhaps because of his two months of illness, Trenchard did not know how forcibly Ellington had spoken out against the proposal for the Route in the autumn of 1918. In essence, Ellington had said:

> As a practical means of delivering machines to Salonika and the Middle East I do not think the scheme has anything to commend it. The estimate of 6 days for the journey is absurd. We took 5 days to get Handley Pages to the Independent Air Force in Eastern France. Even Borton took 10 days to get to Cairo in perfect weather. The scheme is a little ahead of its time. Based on our experience of sending DH 9s to the Independent Air Force in France we can expect to lose most of our planes en route and the duration is likely to be about 25 days not 6.

Ellington was by this time Comptroller General of Equipment. By appointing him as president, Trenchard prevented him from speaking out as a witness, or even muttering 'I told you so'. By appointing Borton as a member he was choosing the man who had pioneered the Route and had earlier concluded that:

> A ferry service of machines to the Middle East should prove a perfectly simple and feasible undertaking.

Neither of these men can be considered as having had nothing to do with No. 1 Aerial Route – quite the reverse. One had been strongly against it and the other had been strongly in favour. They should both have been witnesses and not members of the Court of Enquiry.

The third member that Trenchard proposed was Air Commodore H.R.H. Brooke-Popham, Director of Personnel. He appears to have been an independent choice but by no means satisfied the requirement of severed connections with the RAF. He had learned to fly at Brooklands in 1911 and therefore possessed Royal Aeronautical Club Flying Certificate No. 108. Possession of these early certificates was invaluable for subsequent promotion because they were proof of seniority. He commanded the first aeroplane company of the RFC before the war and the RFC in France before Trenchard took over. He was an Air Commodore by 1919 and retired as an Air Chief Marshal in 1937. He was recalled in 1940 and made Commander in Chief of British Forces in the Far East. This was the first time that an air officer had been given such a senior appointment but equality of status between the three Services made it politically necessary. Japan had not yet entered the war and, like his predecessors, he failed to see the possibility of a Japanese attack from the jungles of Malaya. He had the good fortune to be replaced by Field Marshal Wavell and retired to England just before the Japanese arrived. His *Times* obituary in 1953 does not mention his Singapore appointment. Even *Times* obituaries can be selective.

The final member – very strongly insisted upon, to his credit, by Trenchard – was Mr G.B. Cockburn, one of the fathers of the Royal Naval Air Service. He was the only Briton to fly at the Rheims Air Show in 1909 where he flew in a French Farman, one of the French designs that had already outclassed the Wright Flyer. He had declined a commission in the RNAS and the RAF, preferring to remain a civilian. In 1919 he was in charge of the Aeronautical Inspection Department of the Air Ministry and his civilian status gave him a certain independence of mind. He was looked upon as the elder statesman of the committee since he really was a pioneer airman and, indeed, his evidence helped to put events into perspective.

The civil servants responsible for setting up the enquiry assumed that someone's head would roll, in order to assuage public opinion. Since it was to be a Court of Enquiry they took counsel's advice on procedure, particularly in so far as it might involve civilians, who would not be subject to military law.

However strange things happened in the week following Trenchard's initial proposal to General Seely. Trenchard must have realized that a public enquiry would at least reveal bad management and he was the senior manager concerned.

Director of Training and Organisation to Director of Personnel:

Trenchard now thinks that a legally constituted Court of Enquiry is unnecessary. The terms of reference are to be:

1. Investigate the circumstances under which No. 1 Aerial Route was organised.
2. Make full enquiries into the organisation and working of the route.

3. Investigate fully the causes of the large number of crashes and forced landings that have occurred on this route.

The Director of Training and Organisation was Group Captain Game and he was the man in the Air Ministry to whom McLaren reported.

What had changed Trenchard's mind about a *Court* of Enquiry? The significance of the change is that no judge will be involved and the subject can be thrashed out in private behind closed doors in the Air Ministry. Perhaps some of those who feared that they might be criticized for their part in the project had also expressed their concern to Trenchard.

Cockburn was a civilian but as virtually the father of the Royal Naval Air Service, which had sponsored Handley Page to design and construct the machines at the centre of the enquiry, his discretion and loyalty to the RAF were not in doubt.

The wording of Trenchard's letter to General Seely on 2 October suggests that his first intentions had been to get to the heart of the matter as objectively as possible. But if pinning down responsibility was intended, it didn't happen.

Seely could not be blamed personally for what had gone wrong but as the only politician in Parliament with full-time responsibility for the RAF, he might be called upon to make a symbolic resignation.

Game is not on record as supporting the proposal before the Route was inaugurated but he was Director of Organization and directly responsible for McLaren's work when the Air Route was inaugurated.

John Salmond, like Game, does not appear to have been an enthusiast for the project beforehand. But he had more responsibility than anyone else for the condition of the aircraft and the selection of the crews before they set off.

He was Geoffrey's brother and Geoffrey, as the prime mover of No. 1 Aerial Route, would have to take some responsibility. Geoffrey was based in Cairo and not in a strong position to influence the planning of the route at the Air Ministry. Geoffrey and John between them ran the Air Force in France, Germany and the Middle East. It would be impolitic of Trenchard to upset them. John Laffin, in his biography of John Salmond, hints at strained relations between John Salmond and Trenchard from time to time.[2]

P.R.C. Groves was in favour of the Route in 1918 and he was Director of Flying Operations at the time that it was proposed. He was still in the Air Ministry at the time of the Enquiry but as a supporter of Sykes he did not remain there for long and was retired in 1922. He could hardly escape some responsibility for the inadequacy of the preparations for flying the Route but between the Route's conception in August 1918 and the take-off of 58 Squadron in May 1919, the major changes in responsibility already described, had occurred.

The part-time Secretary of State for the Air, Winston Churchill, is the last person to be considered. He and Trenchard had been fighting to keep the RAF intact while the Army and Navy made repeated attempts to swallow it on the grounds of economy. Churchill had lost his job as First Lord of the Admiralty in 1915 because of the Gallipoli fiasco and he would not want to lose another job as a Secretary of State because of the bad organization of No. 1 Aerial Route. More bad publicity was the last thing he wanted and it would have been easy for him to persuade Trenchard that he too should seek to avoid publicity, for the sake of his own and the RAF's fledgling reputations.

However it came about, the terms of reference were changed and the wisdom of the decision to fly the machines to Cairo instead of shipping them was never questioned throughout the Enquiry. Ellington, who had correctly forecast the likely outcome of the project when it was first proposed, must have had extraordinary self-control or perhaps he realized that to say 'I told you so' might hamper his future career in the RAF. So he *did not* speak out and he *did* become Chief of the Air Staff after Trenchard and the Salmond brothers had taken their turns. One may speculate that the four of them arranged this in private before the Enquiry began. A later event strengthens this speculation.

The first witness was Group Captain P.D. Game, Director of Training and Organization, who was Squadron Leader McLaren's boss and therefore in the direct line of responsibility. He knew Trenchard well. Game had been GSO1 to Trenchard in the RFC in France in 1916 and continued in this job when John Salmond took over from Trenchard in 1918.

169

Phillip Game was followed by the Deputy Comptroller of Equipment, Wing Commander Courteney. He took the place of his boss, Air Vice Marshal Ellington, who was Chairman of the Enquiry. Although not responsible for the aircraft handed over to the route from the squadrons in France, the Equipment Division was responsible for the aircraft supplied from stock in England and for the provision of equipment, tools, spares and transport along the route.

Obviously, Squadron Leader McLaren was called to give his version of events. He must have travelled to London with some trepidation since his original summons was to a 'Court of Enquiry' and he had confessed to Group Captain Game in his letter after the Darley tragedy that 'No. 1 Aerial Route has been a complete failure'. That letter came up in evidence but it probably did him more good than harm. His endeavours to get the machines to Egypt to meet the crisis were never in doubt. Most of the other witnesses were the OCs of the squadrons who flew to Egypt and the OCs of some of the route stations.

Geoffrey Salmond, the man who had so strongly advocated flying the planes rather than shipping them and who had urged the planes forward before adequate preparations had been made, was not called. Neither was his brother, John Salmond, who was sending most of the machines from France. None of them was in the same condition as the machine that Borton had obtained straight from commissioning trials at Martlesham Heath the year before.[3] John Salmond should have known the accident record of machines that were flown from England to France just as well as Ellington knew it. As overall Commander of No. 5 Wing he should also have known how quickly a Handley Page deteriorates with use and with standing around in bad weather. Some of the machines that set off for Egypt had been in France for nearly a year and they were worn out. Because aeroplanes had to be lightweight to be lifted by primitive aero engines, they were fragile and they all had short lives. This was just as true of the Handley Page as it was of the Sopwith Camel.

Captain Lewis, who was in charge at Suda Bay, was not called to appear as a witness either although he had earlier left Crete for London in order to give evidence if required.

A final piece of evidence came from Squadron Leader A.M. Wilson, who had taken over from McLaren when McLaren was summoned to London.[4] Wilson's summons to the enquiry was not sent until 10 December and so he arrived at the Air Ministry too late to influence the findings of the committee. The committee had in any case heard most of his criticisms from other sources. He confirmed that no machines had been given an escort over the Mediterranean since July and made the additional point that it would have been wise to arrange for thorough scheduled overhauls of each plane, regardless of its apparent condition, after each long flight and particularly at Pisa and Taranto, which were well equipped for it. This was the very point that Major Gilley had made to Major McLaren when 58 Squadron was en route. Because he refused to order his crews to fly on without a scheduled service, McLaren sacked him.

No evidence was taken from any of the mechanics such as Sergeant Aspley or Air Mechanic West, which was fortunate for the reputation of those officers who had dallied en route.

The evidence, as it appears from the minutes of the committee meetings, consists of a series of criticisms mostly from the squadrons who flew the route, but also from Squadron Leader McLaren, which were in turn answered by those criticized. Here is a consolidated summary:

Delays caused by lack of spare parts Equipment Division received no requests for them until July. Based on the experience of Brigadier Borton, it was thought that each plane would get through on its own provided that it was in good condition at the start and took the right spares with it. When experience showed this not to be the case an establishment of spares to be held at Route Stations was published in August but that was too late to be of any use.

Poor service from fitters and riggers at Route Stations. Because of demobilization there was a desperate shortage of experienced men. Those that were any good were still with the squadrons in France and flew in the planes that made the journey. Some of the men at the route stations, who were fitters on paper, had never even seen a Rolls-Royce engine. Only two of those posted to the route stations regarded themselves as experienced with Rolls-Royce engines. It was recognized that the fitters flying in the planes resented having to work long hours while the route station men did little to help, but it was safer that way.

Lack of maps. T.E. Lawrence had complained about this when he arrived in Egypt. One crew found its way using a coloured postcard.

Poor reception service from officers in charge of route stations. Much of this criticism resulted from there being no one in authority on

The Handley Page O/400 was powered by two 275hp V12 Rolls-Royce Eagle engines. Maintaining them required more skill than that of an Austin 7 mechanic. (HP808)

the ground when planes arrived. The telegraph service was in many places so poor that ground staff had no idea of either the time or even the day of a plane's arrival. The problem was aggravated by the lack of motor transport. To take Suda Bay as one example, the airfield was no more than a bare field with the accommodation and services at the seaplane station two miles away. There was no motor transport until September and it would not be reasonable to expect an officer to sit in the field all day in case a plane might turn up. Once transport was provided no plane waited more than five minutes for service.

Lack of weather forecasts for the route ahead. Again the poor telegraph services and absence of wireless meant that if planes waited for today's forecast to arrive it was usually too late to start the next leg of the journey. In some cases there was no meteorological station available anyway.

Poor condition of the planes when they joined the route at Buc. 58, 214 and 216 Squadrons had flown very little since the armistice and natural deterioration had occurred. They only had a 'thin veneer' of overhaul before they went to Buc, which was not equipped to give them a thorough overhaul.

Lack of windproof accommodation for machines. Bessoneau hangars were contemplated but there was no time to obtain them before the route commenced and then it did not seem worthwhile, because all was expected to be complete by the end of July. The extra Handley Pages and Vickers Vimys were an afterthought. It might have been different with more warning of the start and of the numbers of planes involved. Extension of the route into the autumn was bound to court trouble with the mistral. Another result of the absence of hangars was that planes stood out in the open in all weathers awaiting repair and getting more unserviceable every day because of rusting control wires, loosening fabric and warping propellers. Even if a plane was superficially undamaged after sitting out in a gale, it would require complete re-rigging.

Carelessness or indifference of pilots with regard to airworthiness of machines, choice of landing places in emergency, over-confidence in not checking head to wind after emergency landings, poor judgement of distances and fuel supply, lateness of departure. These pilots were simply inexperienced. Most of them had no experience other than flying to and from a familiar airfield in England or France, where they had well trained fitters and riggers with the right tools and equipment on hand to look after their machines. They did not have the practical experience of McLaren or the influence of Borton. A quarter of them had only recently been posted to their squadrons when the order came to fly to Buc and then to Cairo.

Chronic trouble with petrol feed systems. The petrol pumps on both Handley Pages and Vickers Vimys were unreliable and needed redesigning. The problem was aggravated because, on the older machines, rubber petrol feed pipes had perished in sunlight so that bits of rubber sometimes blocked pipes or carburettors.

Lack of commitment from the Route Station Officers. The logistical support that they had received was negligible, particularly in the first two months. Some were criticized for poor service before they had even arrived at their posts. Poor communications, lack of transport, poor accommodation, shortage of skilled men, and lack of adequate financial arrangements, all contributed to their problems. The cheques of thirteen pilots bounced at the *Grand Hotel*, Pisa.

Lack of escort flying boats over the Mediterranean. This was because of sickness, shortage of pilots caused by demobilization and greater priorities elsewhere. In the early stages, because of poor communications, flying boats were waiting around doing nothing and deteriorating. Control of the flying boats rested with the AOC RAF Malta and not with McLaren.

Air Vice Marshal E.H. Ellington.   Brigadier 'Biffy' Borton.

Air Vice Marshal Geoffrey Salmond.   Air Marshal John Salmond.

The main conclusions of the investigating committee, para-phrased, were as follows:

1. Six accidents were primarily caused by equipment failure and four by pilot error but the biggest single cause was gale force winds coupled with the lack of hangars.
2. None of the accidents was attributable to bad organization of the route.

This conclusion cleared Squadron Leader McLaren of blame. He could not be blamed without the risk that he would emphasize the pressure he had been under from Geoffrey Salmond. His career in the RAF continued unblemished.

3. 214 Squadron was by far the most successful. The bad state of the machines in the other cases reflects very little credit on the squadrons concerned.
4. The speed with which the operation was mounted accounts for many of the problems but this was a military necessity.

This was the excuse for Geoffrey Salmond. His insistence on 58 Squadron setting off before the servicing airfields had been

175

properly established was unwise but Salmond himself was no doubt under pressure from his army colleagues in Cairo. The decision to fly rather than ship the machines was a serious mistake but this point was not made in the Committee's conclusions.

5. A significant contribution came from Mr Cockburn who arranged for a comparison of the accidents on this route compared with accidents to the Handley Pages that were flown to Eastern France for the Independent Air Force to bomb Germany in the last six months of the war.

	No. 1 Aerial Route	Ferry to France
Miles flown	28,443	93,110
Number of machines	278	51
Number of accidents	4	10 (gales excluded)
Miles per accident	7,111	9,311

He also pointed out that the average life of machines in service in France in 1918 had been only sixty-one flying hours and that only one-third of replacements were due to enemy action. For planning purposes the squadrons in France in 1918 budgeted to lose about a third of their machines by accidents and deterioration each month.[5] Despite their size, these Handley Page bombers were fragile. This is exactly the point that Ellington had made when he advised against the Aerial Route a year before.

6. Eight lives were lost, four in one machine. These losses of men and machines were inevitable with the state of aeronautical development at the time. The use of the word 'inevitable' sounds callous but the RAF was used to high casualty figures. During 1918 about 100 pilots a month were killed in training and in the year following the Armistice another 126 aircrew were killed. Flying was still a dangerous occupation.[6]

7. There is an urgent need to persuade foreign governments to change from telegraph to wireless as a means of long distance communication.

Studying the story of No. 1 Aerial Route today it is impossible to avoid the conclusion that Geoffrey Salmond was unrealistic in his assertion that delivery by air was preferable to delivery by ship. The facts prove that he was wrong and that Ellington was right. More planes would have reached Egypt, and reached it sooner, if they had been sent by sea instead of by air. They would also have arrived in better condition. Most of the machines that did arrive safely in Heliopolis were written off as too worn out to fly further.

Notes

1. Air 2/113/A29644.
2. John Laffin op.cit. p.147, pp.211–212.
3. Both Salmonds had exchanged the rank of Major General for Air Vice Marshal three months before the Enquiry.
4. Air 2/107/A17762.
5. Air 1/70/15/9/122.
6. Air 2/114/A34172, Air 1/474/15/312/185.

CHAPTER 14

The Aftermath

Despite the assurances given to Parliament by General Seely that 'the fullest enquiries would be made and that if it was found that mistakes had been made, appropriate action would be taken', no one, save perhaps Seely himself, suffered for his part in the project. 'Overriding military necessity' justified everything.

Seely did resign. If more questions had been asked in Parliament or if the press had decided to pursue the story further, he would have been standing on thin ice because of the change in the terms of reference for the Enquiry compared with what he had promised in Parliament. His resignation came some weeks before the report was put before the Air Council but at about the time that the committee finished its work. He claimed that his resignation had nothing to do with the aerial route. He was simply piqued that the jobs of Secretary of State for War and Secretary of State for Air had been merged under Winston Churchill, which he feared was a threat to the existence of a separate Air Ministry.[1]

This explanation is not completely convincing because Churchill had held the combined post for more than a year and had already demonstrated that he had no thought of returning the Air Force to Army or Navy control. It would be to Seely's credit if his conscience was troubled. Ellington was put in an invidious, or just possibly, comfortable position when he was appointed Chairman of the Enquiry. It ensured that he would not have to rock the boat by pointing out that he had foreseen the tragedy and advised against the project. Seely, the Under Secretary of State for Air, must have supported Ellington's appointment as chairman, unless of course someone senior to him such as the Secretary of State for Air was handling the politics of the situation.

Seely had resigned once before to shield others. He had been Secretary of State for War in 1914 when the Asquith government tried to force through Home Rule for all Ireland. Ulster Protestant Irishmen were prominent in the British Army and they made it plain that they were not prepared to use force against the new paramilitary Ulster Volunteer Force. The incident became known as 'the Curragh Mutiny'. Earl Kitchener and Sir John French gave in to the rebel officers, amongst whom was General Gough, one of Haig's Army Commanders. The 'rebellion' caused a furore in Parliament. General Seely took the blame and resigned to protect Kitchener and French who were needed for the war about to commence. Did he also resign on this 1919 occasion to protect Trenchard or even Churchill? We shall never know.

If Seely was a man of principle, the wisdom of his resignation on this second occasion would have been confirmed by what happened to the Enquiry report after it was finished. Air Vice Marshal Ellington, as Chairman of the Enquiry, sent it to the Air Council on 22 January 1920. G. Hutchins, who signs himself in the Air Ministry files as 'S5', read it and next day wrote a note on the manila cover of the file:

> Considerable interest was aroused in the Press and Parliament about these accidents. I do not think it can be said that a definite promise was made to make the findings of the committee public unless the first sentence of General Seely's reply on the 28th of October can be taken to mean this.[2]

A little further down on the same manila file cover Hutchins records an extract from the minutes of the Air Council meeting on 2 February, which simply says that the Air Council has approved the Enquiry report. If the members of the Air Council made any comments about it during the meeting they were not recorded here.

Below that comment and still on the file cover, there is the following comment:

> This may go by.
>
> WarC. 4.2.20

The entry written on the manila cover of the Enquiry file.

It took me some time to work out who had written his initials under the comment 'this may go by' but I finally discovered that 'WarC' was how Churchill initialled his correspondence at the time. He was, after all, Secretary of State for War as well as Secretary of State for the Air and he was busy fighting the Bolsheviks. It was a typical Churchillian gesture. He chose this warlike title presumably because it pleased him.

We shall never know what Ellington's innermost thoughts were about No. 1 Aerial Route. The second note on this same file (next page), but not made until 23 January 1924, states that certain papers concerning No. 1 Aerial Route have been extracted from Sir Edward Ellington's private file on the subject. One might suppose that they were transferred to the Enquiry file but there

MINUTE SHEET.   Air Ministry File No.

is nothing there that is not already in one or another of the half dozen files about No. 1 Aerial Route. Perhaps these papers were too embarrassing and they were destroyed. They might have revealed an agreement that Ellington should have a turn as Chief of the Air Staff as a reward for keeping quiet about his accurate forecast in late 1918 of what would happen if so many planes tried to fly No. 1 Aerial Route in the state of aviation knowledge at the time.

If the report had reached the Press and if the Press had been as keen to expose Government wrongdoing as it is nowadays, it would have been called a whitewash. But it did not reach the Press and the reputations of all concerned remained intact.

We need be in no doubt what the Secretary of State for Air had in mind when he wrote 'This may go by'. It also explains why my search for newspaper reports about the Enquiry findings has been fruitless. Churchill and Trenchard decided to try to conceal the findings of the Enquiry from Parliament and from the public.

It was three months since the Darley disaster hit the headlines. The newspapers forgot to follow up the story and the Air Ministry did nothing to remind them. Churchill and Trenchard's gamble paid off.

In a clever move, just at the time when the Enquiry Report might have been expected, Trenchard published instead his White Paper on The Permanent Organisation of the RAF (Cmd 467). This attracted much attention and devotees of Trenchard still regard it as the most important document ever published about the future planning of the RAF. It contained lots of good things but it advocated an air force with no bombers at all because Trenchard thought that they were a 'waste of time'.[3] This was also Field Marshal Haig's view and Trenchard worshipped Haig.[4] He owed his advancement to him.

The senior RAF officers involved in No. 1 Aerial Route took it in turns to be Chief of the Air Staff and they were all knighted later in their careers. Like Trenchard, they were all from the RFC and no representative of the Admiralty point of view about aviation policy ever got a look in.[5] John Salmond succeeded Trenchard and was succeeded in turn by his brother Geoffrey in 1933. Geoffrey succeeded his brother in a hurry in 1933 because Geoffrey had been diagnosed with cancer. The pact that I suggest the four of them had made at the time of the Enquiry had to be honoured so John resigned to give Geoffrey his turn as Chief of the Air Staff before it was too late. This kind gesture suggests that the succession had been 'fixed' some time before. Geoffrey died only a month later and John returned to the job temporarily until Ellington was available to take his turn. Ellington remained Chief of the Air Staff until 1937.

An incident in 1937 suggests that Ellington was only made CAS reluctantly, so far as Trenchard was concerned. The Admiralty was pressing hard for aeroplanes based on aircraft carriers to be returned to Admiralty control as the Fleet Air Arm. In Trenchard's opinion Ellington was not aware of what was going on politically and was therefore making too little effort to prevent it. At a garden party at Buckingham Palace in the summer of 1937 Ellington commented that he thought the RAF had a good case for maintaining the status quo. Trenchard cut him short and was overheard to say:

> Do you never leave your office Ellington? The thing's over. It's
> been decided over your head, which is well-buried in the sand
> as usual.[6]

This is not the kind of remark that one would expect from a so-
called 'Father of the RAF' who had any respect for this successor
of his as CAS. I again suggest that Ellington became CAS because
he had agreed in 1919 to protect Churchill, Trenchard and the
Salmond brothers' reputations over the No. 1 Aerial Route debacle.
Perhaps he would never have reached the top otherwise.

* * *

The eighteen-year period from the appointment of Trenchard
to the retirement of Ellington is marked by a serious decline in
the size and capability of the RAF compared with the air forces
of other major powers. It is customary to blame this on British
pacifism but one can at least observe that the Chiefs of the Air
Staff lacked influence. None of them thought of resigning in
protest against government-imposed economies. A man of the
calibre of General Allenby might have made a difference but the
RAF didn't have one. The one man who would certainly have
ensured the survival of bomber development in the RAF in the
post-war years was that stalwart of the RNAS, Admiral Kerr. He
was the man who in 1917 had pointed out the need for a
retaliatory bomber force and his paper to the War Cabinet on this
subject led to the formation of the RAF despite protests from
Trenchard and Haig. Trenchard got rid of Kerr as soon as he
could once the war was over and until World War Two top jobs in
the RAF were filled by pilots from the old RFC who had learned
to fly before 1915.

Trenchard was CAS for eleven years and he made a bad start
by abolishing bombers altogether despite the wealth of evidence
from both London and the Rhineland of the drastic effect of bombing on civilian morale in 1917 and 1918. Five years later, in 1923,
he saw the error of his ways and there was talk of building up the
bomber force again, but nothing effective was done. Even British
civil airliners, lacking government financial support, were pathetic
compared with German, Dutch and American competitors. In his
interview with Trenchard, when he offered him Sykes' post as

The Handley Page Heyford was first supplied to the RAF in 1933. It was Britain's front-line bomber in 1937. It was mostly canvas and wood with open cockpits. 120 were built and they never saw active service because they were no match for the Heinkel, Dornier and Junkers JU52 and 87.

CAS, Churchill proclaimed that 'civil aviation must fly by itself'. Most of the aviation development staff who had put Britain in the lead in 1918 had disappeared. A few did remain and we have them to thank for the Hurricane and the Spitfire.

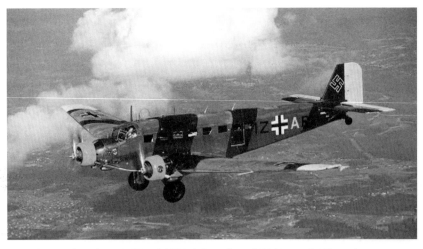

The all-metal Junkers JU52 of 1931. More than 5,000 were built and some were still in service in the Swiss Air Force in 1980.

As far as bombers were concerned the situation was hopeless compared with Germany until 1939. Barnes Wallis designed the twin-engined Vickers Wellington with its damage resistant geodesic canvas-covered framework, but although twin-engined bombers could reach England easily from France, four-engined machines were needed to reach Germany from England with a worthwhile load of bombs and adequate navigation equipment. The first really successful British bomber – the four-engined Avro Lancaster – was not brought into service until 1942 and by then Britain had suffered the Blitz without being able to retaliate effectively.

* * *

Group Captain Groves did not resign but he did retire in 1922 when he was still in his early forties. He had supported Sykes' plan for seventeen squadrons of bombers to be maintained in the post-war air force and he regarded Trenchard's plans for the RAF as disastrous. He left the RAF in order to be free to speak out against Trenchard's policy.

Group Captain Game did not become Chief of the Air Staff either, but he went on to become an air vice marshal. Like all the others, he was an early RFC pilot. He was AOC India in 1922 and then Governor of New South Wales. When he returned to England he succeeded his old friend, Trenchard, as Commissioner of the Metropolitan Police where he distinguished himself by preventing Oswald Moseley and the British Union of Fascists from marching down Cable Street in 1936.

Students of Victorian history may also find it intriguing to be told that Game had been the young Artillery subaltern in charge of the gun carriage bearing Queen Victoria's coffin from Windsor railway station to St George's Chapel in January 1901. The horses got out of control and the half-ton coffin nearly fell off the gun carriage. The harness traces were broken and the horses had to be replaced by the sailors who were lining the street. The communication cord from the Royal train, which had brought the coffin from London, was commandeered to give them something to pull with. Since then gun carriages bearing royal coffins have been pulled by teams of sailors and not by horses.

Squadron Leader McLaren did not suffer either. He had already been awarded the Air Force Cross for his part in the first flight to

Egypt and the OBE for his flight to India. In 1924 he organized a round-the-world-flight sponsored by *The Times*. The plane used was a Vickers Vulture flying boat, which set off from Calshot on 25 March. This plane crashed in Burma and was replaced by another that was brought out by ship. But this too crashed on Bering Island, Siberia, in fog. No one was hurt but the flight was abandoned. An American crew succeeded in a Douglas a few weeks later.

There was also recognition for some of the aircrews who had pioneered the world's first long-distance air route.

> Air Vice Marshal W.G.H. Salmond, to Director of Personnel. 27.1.20.
>
> I suggest that a certain number of awards should be given to the most deserving cases of all officers who flew out machines from England to Egypt during 1919 and that the case of Lt. Yates and Lt. Vance should be considered with them. If this is agreed to I will forward the names in due course.

Air Commodore Brooke-Popham, who was Director of Personnel, had been on the Enquiry committee so he knew all about No. 1 Aerial Route.

> Director of Personnel to A.V.M. Salmond. 29.1.20.
>
> I agree but will you please keep the number of recommendations as small as possible.

The honours system grinds along slowly and the awards finally appeared in the *London Gazette* on 12 July 1920. The Air Force Cross was awarded to thirteen officers and the Air Force Medal to fifteen riggers and fitters. Henderson, who had initiated the criticism of McLaren for sacking Gilley, was the only squadron leader not to receive a medal.

Notes
1. For the Hansard report of his resignation see *Flight* magazine for 20 November 1919.
2. G. Hutchins was a Temporary Principal in the Department of the Secretary of the Air Council.

3. Excerpt from Trenchard's diary for 11 November 1918.
4. Boyle op.cit p.178.
5. In fairness, the RFC was four times larger than the RNAS but that does not justify complete exclusion of the RNAS from the top appointment. Hindsight shows that RNAS strategy at the time, which saw a major role for strategic bombing, was wiser than that of the RFC.
6. Boyle op.cit. p. 701. The Fleet Air Arm was, in fact, returned to Admiralty control in May 1939.

CHAPTER 15

England to Australia – the Competition

The preparations for the presumed Court of Enquiry began in October 1919. While this was happening an exciting development was underway in London, which arose directly from the experience gained on No. 1 Aerial Route.

Encouraged by the string of airfields that had been established all the way from London to Calcutta, thanks largely to Borton, it was decided that there should be a competition to see who could be the first to fly to Australia. The pioneering flights from England to Cairo and from Cairo to India have already been described and so has the reconnoitering by ship of the route as far as Timor by Borton and Smith.

This reconnaissance occupied the winter of 1918–1919. Because of the destruction of C9700 at Risalpur and the deployment of C9681 in Egypt, they no longer had a machine for their intended flight, so they returned to England, which they reached in September 1919. When they arrived they heard all about the competition to fly to Australia.

There is, however, the possibility that Ross Smith already knew about this project because he may have been involved in plans for the competition without Biffy Borton's knowledge.

The Australian Prime Minister, Billy Hughes, was in Europe for the Paris Peace Conference and was one of the many VIPs who flew between Hendon (London) and Buc (Paris) in the Handley

Pages of No. 1 Communications Squadron of the RAF. He rapidly became a flying enthusiast.

According to Hughes' account, he visited wounded Australian soldiers quartered in Cobham Hall, Kent and there met some Australian airmen who wanted the chance to fly back to Australia instead of going back by ship. Since a machine for the purpose, together with all the logistical support, would cost at least £15,000 there was no way in which they could finance this out of their own pockets. So they suggested that the Australian Government should finance it, including the purchase of the machines, which would revert to Government use when they reached their destination. They would be useful for mapping the outback. Alternatively, perhaps commercial sponsors could be found.

On 18 February Hughes sent the following telegram to his cabinet colleagues in Melbourne (Canberra was not created until 1927).

> Several Australian aviators are desirous of attempting flight London to Australia in a Handley Page machine. They are all first class men and very keen … It would be a great advertisement for Australia and would concentrate the eyes of the world upon us if the flight were undertaken.

He went on to point out that a prize of £10,000 was being offered for the first plane to fly the Atlantic and that therefore a similar prize should be offered for the first successful flight *by Australians* to Australia.

A month later the Acting Prime Minister in Australia made the following announcement in the House of Representatives:

> With a view to stimulating aerial activity, the Commonwealth Government has decided to offer £10,000 for the first successful flight to Australia from Great Britain, in a machine manned by Australians. The rules and conditions governing the contest are now being drawn up, and it is proposed that competitors be required to supply their own machines and to make all other necessary arrangements in connection with the flight.

Of course none of the airmen involved could afford to finance the flight themselves. They were dependent on commercial sponsorship, which came, somewhat reluctantly, from the aircraft manufacturers.

But why all this insistence on a plane manned by Australians? The idea for the £10,000 prize had been copied from the *Daily Mail's* initiative for the first Atlantic crossing. But in that case the prize would go to whoever made the crossing regardless of nationality. In stipulating 'Australians only' the government in Melbourne ran the risk of being made a laughing stock by having a non-Australian crew arrive first. Indeed that nearly did happen, as we shall see later.

There are two possible explanations, one of which is that the all-Australian crew stipulation was the idea of the Australian airmen awaiting repatriation at Cobham Hall in Kent. The other explanation is offered here.

Ross Smith had a brother – Keith Smith – who had paid his own passage to England in 1917 and learned to fly in the RAF. By the end of the war he was a flying instructor. He was not smothered with decorations for flying exploits like his younger brother Ross but he was, nevertheless, a competent pilot and a good navigator. In the spring of 1919 he too was waiting to be shipped back to Australia. No doubt he would prefer to fly if given the chance.

In January 1919 Ross Smith was in India with the experience of the flight from Cairo under his belt and with the knowledge that Brigadier Borton had experienced no trouble in his earlier flight from England to Cairo in the previous August. Ross Smith and Borton both knew that a flight to Australia was within sight.

At this stage then, it is at least possible, if not probable, that Ross thought about his brother, Keith, in England and how disappointed Keith would be if Ross flew to Australia without him. Ross would also have known that the very approachable Prime Minister of Australia, Billy Hughes, was accessible in London or Paris because of the Paris Peace Conference. There was nothing to prevent Ross from sending telegrams from Delhi or Calcutta to both his brother and Hughes explaining the situation and saying that the flight to Australia was bound to be undertaken by Borton and himself unless the Australian Government could put up the prize money with the condition of an all-Australian crew attached to it. By this means Ross could displace Borton and bring his brother into the team, together with the two Australian mechanics who had flown the Cairo-Calcutta trip. If Ross felt that such a telegram was a bit bold and blunt to send direct to his Prime Minister then he could have sent it to his older brother in England and entrusted him with the delicate task of approaching Hughes about it.

The evidence for this is circumstantial but there was an obvious motive and the timing of events suits. Ross Smith and Brigadier Borton arrived at Calcutta on 12 December and sailed from Calcutta on 10 February. If Ross Smith was going to send telegrams he could have done it at any time between those two dates. Prime Minister Hughes sent his telegram to his Cabinet in Australia on 18 February. He thus had plenty of time to think over Ross Smith's proposition, if one had been made.

Hughes stated that the idea for the all-Australian crew emanated from Australian airmen that he met at Cobham Hall, Kent, on Christmas Day 1918. But Nelson Eustis, the author of the principal book on the England to Australia Air Race, states:

> I have been unable to trace the several Australian aviators desirous of attempting the flight to Australia mentioned in Hughes' cable.[1]

Eustis did four years' research for this book, which was published in 1968 and he had been studying Australian aviation himself since 1930. So perhaps the suggestion of an all-Australian crew came from Ross Smith and not from some anonymous airmen at Cobham Hall. If the suggestion had come from Ross Smith, he would be the one most likely to link it to the use of a Handley Page, which is what Hughes did in his telegram to Australia. Australians had mostly served in fighter squadrons and knew little about Handley Pages. When the entries in the race became known only one was based on the use of a Handley Page and that entry was Ross Smith's. Yet Billy Hughes had mentioned specifically the Handley Page and no other machine by name in his memo to his government on 18 February. Someone put the idea of a Handley Page into his head and that was probably Ross Smith or his brother.

Nelson Eustis, who was an Australian, goes on to say in his book:

It certainly could not have been Ross Smith (who made the suggestion), because it was his intention, after completing the ship survey, to return to Lahore, where they had left the Handley Page. It was from here that General Borton and Ross Smith intended to fly to Australia, using the landing strips and facilities that they had established.

But the survey and the supplies that they were planning to set out along the route would have been just as useful for a fresh flight from England, with Keith Smith on board, as they would be for a continued flight from India with General Borton on board. From Smith's point of view, a fresh flight from England would now have the added attraction of the prize money, for which a flight with Borton would not be eligible. Ross Smith might have been thinking along these lines even if Borton wasn't.

It is difficult now to study the characters of Ross Smith and Biffy Borton but they certainly had different backgrounds. Biffy Borton's father's diaries have been edited and printed by his step grandson Guy Slater.[2] The diaries depict a leading family of the upper middle class. They had an estate at Cheveney near Yalding in Kent, and they played their part in ruling the Empire.

Cheveney, Yalding, Kent. This was the home of Lieutenant Colonel A.C. Borton JP. He was the squire of the village and both his sons were brought up there. His older son won the VC in Palestine and his younger son, Brigadier Borton, was the first man to fly an aeroplane to Egypt. This son inherited the property from his father and lived there after the Great War. He became an Air Vice Marshal and commuted in his light aeroplane from Cheveney to the Air Ministry in London until his retirement in 1933. He lived on at Cheveney until 1969. (CS)

Biffy's grandfather had been Governor of Malta, his father's cousin was Postmaster General of Egypt and last, but not least, Biffy's brother had won the VC in Palestine. Biffy had an Eton and Black Watch background and usually wore a monocle. He succeeded to the estate in 1927 and he maintained its traditions. Guy Slater, his step-grandson, can remember, as a teenager, dressing for dinner in the 1950s but later the same evening being sent to his room by Biffy for passing the port in the wrong direction. In his commentary to the diaries referred to above, Guy summed up the Borton family as follows:

> They are brave, generous and charming: They are also elitist, intolerant and unthinking. The private virtues and the public vices of the High Tory ...
>
> ... The modesty, the courtesy, the courage and the kindness are real and touching. But I do not think it should blind one to the almost wilful ignorance these people display to the realities of the world outside their magic circle of upper class Anglo-Saxons.

Did Ross Smith really want to be seen as co-pilot to a man with this background? That the two became good friends during their flying days is well attested. But Ross Smith was from a sheep farming business in Adelaide. Even allowing for Adelaide's reputation as the most British of Australian cities, it was on the opposite side of the world, literally and metaphorically. We know that Ross Smith admired Borton's ability but he must have wondered how such an ill-assorted pair as Borton and himself would be received in Australia, should they ever get that far. As a result of the heavy loss of Australian and New Zealand lives in the Gallipoli fiasco, which had been led by British generals, upper class Pommy generals were not popular down under and Borton was just such an individual.[3]

And why did Nelson Eustis make the statement in his book that it certainly could not have been Ross Smith who made the suggestion to insist on an all Australian crew? And why did he feel the need to insert the word 'certainly' into the sentence in which he exonerates Ross Smith from taking part in a plan to ensure an all-Australian crew? Reference has already been made to Major McLaren's use of the word 'undoubtedly' in a situation where there was obviously room for doubt. One can be forgiven for thinking that the same may apply to Eustis Nelson's use of 'certainly' in this case. It is even possible that Eustis had himself thought of the interpretation of events advanced here and was trying to protect the reputations of both Ross Smith and Prime Minister Hughes. However understandable it may have been for the Australians to cut Borton out, it was bad luck for him. He would have enjoyed a knighthood. It would have matched his brother's VC.

Prime Minister Billy Hughes himself might well have been one who did not instinctively warm to an Eton schoolboy who had risen to be a brigadier and usually wore a monocle. Hughes admired much about British tradition. He had even damaged his own career by campaigning for conscription in Australia. But he detested the system that marked people such as Haig for top jobs in the establishment. Hughes' father had been a carpenter in the Houses of Parliament and his mother a housemaid in London. His mother died when he was seven and in 1884 he emigrated to Australia on an assisted passage. By 1890 he was a militant and successful dockers' leader in Sydney and was elected to the New South Wales Parliament in 1894. In 1917 he became Prime Minister of the Federal Parliament and was back in England by

Billy Hughes, Prime Minister of Australia, visiting his troops in France in the autumn of 1918. He stayed on for the Paris Peace Conference in 1919. (Q605)

late 1918. At the Peace Conference his wisecracks infuriated the leading delegates but delighted lesser mortals who were attending. His whole life centred on support for the underdog against those who were unfairly privileged.

Hughes had yet another axe to grind. This concerned trade relations between Britain and Australia. Imperial preference had been a political issue in both countries since the turn of the century. Hughes, naturally, was in favour of duty-free preference for trade between the two countries and felt that it was Australia's due after the part Australian volunteers had played in winning the war. But the British Prime Minister Lloyd George was a Liberal and would have none of Hughes' demands for imperial preference. Australians had fought well in France and at Gallipoli (some say that they had more guts than their British partners) and it was in adversity at Gallipoli that a true Australian national spirit had been forged. These were recent events and provided more reasons for Hughes to favour an all-Australian project. Australians who were national heroes, worthy of having statues erected in their honour, were in short supply because the nation was so young.

However it came about, by the time Borton and Ross Smith returned to England in mid-September 1919, the Australian Government's offer of a £10,000 prize for an all-Australian crew was an established fact. The Royal Aero Club had set out the rules of the competition and entries were already being received. Borton was disappointed at this turn of events, but he was not heartbroken. While in India at the end of the proving flight he had met his future wife, Muriel Slater, who was to be Guy Slater's grandmother. Biffy was already middle aged and Muriel, a widow, had four young children from a previous marriage. Long-distance flying was dangerous and he may have thought that it was time to settle down. Whatever his feelings, he now loyally used his influence and experience to make the contest a success and in particular to help the Smith brothers.

The first entry was received even before the competition rules had been published. It was from a Queenslander called Bert Hinckler but he wanted to fly solo and the rules prevented this on safety grounds. Nine years later he had his way and made the first solo flight from England to Australia.

The competition rules were announced on 25 May 1919. Amongst many other things, they stipulated that no machine could start before 8 September in order to give time for adequate preparation of airfields. This precaution may well have been introduced as a result of the experience of No. 1 Aerial Route. Shell agreed to arrange the distribution of petrol along the route and Wakefield Ltd provided the oil. Time was also needed to obtain permission for overflights from the countries along the route.

The second entry, on 26 May, was from Valdemar Rendle in a Blackburn Kangaroo. There were lengthy negotiations about the composition of the crew because the Royal Aero Club had doubts about their navigational experience. But eventually the crew was agreed as Captain G.H. Wilkins, navigator, Lieutenant V. Rendle, pilot, Lieutenant D.R. Williams, 2nd pilot, and Lieutenant G.H.M. St Clair-Potts, mechanic.

The third entry, on 24 June, was from Lieutenant Raymond Parer and Lieutenant J.C. McIntosh. Negotiations for an aeroplane were protracted and they didn't set off in their DH9 until the winners had finished the course and the race was over.

The fourth entry, on 3 August, was from Captain R.M. Douglas and Lieutenant J.S.L. Ross in a single-engined Alliance machine that was called *The Endeavour* as a tribute to Captain Cook.

On 11 August a Frenchman called Etienne Poulet and his mechanic, Jean Benoist, announced that they were going to fly from Paris to Australia in a twin-engined Caudron GIV. They were not eligible for the competition because of their nationality, but they intended to leave before the agreed start of the race and to get there first.

On 15 August entry number six came from Captain Cedric Howell and air mechanic George Fraser. They intended to fly in a Martinsyde A1.

Entry number seven came on 16 September when the Sopwith Aviation Company nominated Captain G.C. Matthews and Sergeant T.D. Kay to fly their Sopwith Strutter called the *Wallaby*.

There was still no entry from the Smith brothers but on 19 September General Borton presented his report on the survey of the route from Calcutta to East Timor. Most of the crews attended this meeting. The route laid down from London to Calcutta was obviously the route that Borton and McLaren had pioneered, taking full advantage of the facilities of No. 1 Aerial

Route as far as Cairo, and then the Borton and Smith route via Baghdad to Calcutta. At that stage no airfields had been selected for the final 1,750 miles between Singapore and Darwin but this was sorted out before the race began.

The Frenchman Poulet, in the twin-engined Caudron, left Villers Coublay, Paris, on 14 October and flew in terrible weather, with many delays via Salonika, Constantinople, Syria, Baghdad, Karachi, and Delhi. By the time he reached Delhi he knew that he was being closely pursued and he pressed on as fast as he could to Calcutta and Rangoon. His was the leading plane until Calcutta and he commanded the headlines in the Australian newspapers. But the Caudron came to grief after Rangoon with a broken propeller and a cracked piston. Poulet retired. The Frenchman came close to confounding them all. If he had arrived first, what would have happened to the £10,000 prize?

Last, but by no means least, on 18 October, the race favourites entered: the Smith brothers with their mechanics, Shiers and Bennett. In the light of experience, a Vickers Vimy was now their preferred machine for the flight. Crucially, it could carry enough fuel for thirteen hours' flying whereas the Handley Page ran dry after only ten. Once again, the loyal support of Borton stands out. In Ross Smith's own words:

> In mid September we arrived back in England. I at once got in touch with Messrs. Vickers Ltd., and asked them if they would supply a machine for the flight. This they refused to do at first. General Borton however, pointed out to them that I had been practically over the entire route and had done a great deal of long distance flying. They reconsidered their decision and consented to furnish the machine. Once Vickers decided, they entered whole-heartedly into the project.[4]

Brigadier Borton must have realized by now that the success of his flight to Cairo in 1918 was largely due to obtaining a brand-new machine straight from the factory and he made sure that the Smith brothers had the same advantage. They spent a month with the machine and its manufacturers before they took delivery.

The Australian Flying Corps sergeants, Shiers and Bennett, who had flown with Borton and Smith to India, were the obvious choice as mechanics. So the all-Australian crew was assembled and Vickers lent the machine. Not only did they lend the machine, they also fitted it with two Rolls-Royce Eagle Mark VIII engines giving a total of 720 horsepower. Only two other engines of this design had been made and they had been fitted to Alcock and Brown's transatlantic machine earlier in the year.

Notes

1. Nelson Eustis – *The Greatest Air Race – England – Australia 1919.* Angus & Robertson. p. 8. He died in 2003.
2. Guy Slater, *My Warrior Sons, The Borton Family Diary 1914–18,* Peter Davies Ltd, 1973.
3. General Ian Hamilton, Commander of the Allied troops in the Gallipoli landings and a personal friend of Winston Churchill, never put a foot on shore apart from taking tea on the beach one afternoon during a lull in the fighting.
4. Sir Ross Smith KBE MC DFC AFC – *The First Aeroplane Voyage from England to Australia,* Angus & Robertson, Sydney 1920.

CHAPTER 16

The Race – Winners and Losers

The fortuitous existence of No. 1 Aerial Route as far as Cairo looked like being of real benefit to all the crews but the delay in the start date, caused by the need to get the Far Eastern airfields ready with petrol and oil delivered to them, meant that it was not at all clear whether the Aerial Route stations would still be manned by the time the Australian planes reached them. The RAF was anxious to abandon that route and forget all about it.

December 6th. Telegram Air Ministry to Taranto.

Suda Bay to be closed down in accordance with earlier instructions and handed over to Greek Naval Air Service. Please arrange for either Lt. Semple or Captain Lewis to report to Air Ministry with all records. Advise earliest that this can be done.

Presumably the newspapers in England carried news about the preparations for the competition but the first hint of it that appears in the No. 1 Aerial Route correspondence is the following memo from the Air Ministry to Major McLaren.

Approximate dates of departure for Australian flight:

Sopwith	Pilot Matthews	19 Oct
Alliance	Pilot Douglas	29 Oct
Kangaroo	Pilot Rendle	30 Oct
Vimy	Pilot Smith	30 Oct

Instruct all route stations to afford every facility.

These dates proved optimistic. There was no mention of Poulet and Howell because they were not planning to use the Suda Bay airfield. This airfield was the one that the RAF was most anxious to close down because it would be unusable once the rains started. Poulet left on 14 October and flew via Salonika and Constantinople. The war was over and Constantinople had a British garrison. Howell left on 4 December and was intending to follow the same route as Poulet. Parer was omitted because his plans were not yet known.

Matthews and Kay, left Hounslow in the Sopwith Wallaby on 21 October – only two days later than predicted in the Air Ministry memo. Harry Hawker flew alongside them for the first few miles of the journey in a Sopwith Triplane. He had been made famous five months before when he and his co-pilot, Commander Grieve, were rescued from mid-ocean while attempting a transatlantic flight. There was no news of them for several days because the Danish ship that rescued them, the SS *Mary*, had no long-distance radio and they were given up for lost. The SS *Mary* managed to make contact with land as it was passing the north of Scotland and she was met by a British destroyer, which transhipped the two airmen. People cheered as they passed through each railway station on their way south and when they reached London they again faced huge crowds. They both received the Air Force Cross for gallantry from King George V and they also received a cheque for £5,000 from Lord Northcliffe as a consolation prize. Long-distance flying was becoming a national obsession.

The Wallaby crew decided to take the Salonika and Constantinople route and therefore did not feature in the No. 1 Aerial Route correspondence. After various problems, which included four days' imprisonment by Bolsheviks in Yugoslavia, they got as far as Bali in the Dutch East Indies. Here they crashed on 17 April

1920 – beyond repair and long after the winners had reached Australia.

Douglas and Ross in the Alliance *Endeavour* took off from Hounslow at 11.33 a.m. on 13 November. They crashed six minutes later at Surbiton. They were seen coming out of cloud at low altitude in a slow spin, and out of control. The machine crashed heavily. Ross died instantly; Douglas died a few minutes after the arrival of a doctor. No fault could be found with the machine afterwards but there had been major repairs just before the flight. This was probably yet another case of a pilot banking too steeply at low altitude. When in cloud it was exceedingly difficult to judge angles of climbing or banking. Perhaps the Alliance machine was not fitted with a clinometer as Handley Pages were.

On 17 November McLaren, who was now based at Taranto, reported that the airfield at Suda Bay was still in excellent condition, which was lucky for the Smith brothers in the Vickers Vimy because they landed there that afternoon. The Air Ministry files have little information on the subject because these flights were not an RAF responsibility but there are plenty of other accounts – one by Ross Smith in the *National Geographic* magazine in March 1921.

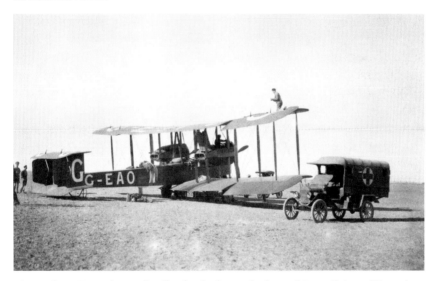

The Vickers Vimy being finally checked over before taking off from Hounslow on 12 December 1919. The U in the registration is obscured by something draped over the fuselage. (Q94252)

They left the snow-covered airfield at Hounslow in Class V weather (unfit for flying) soon after 8 a.m. on 12 November. They climbed through thick cloud but at 2,000 feet reached clear blue skies and flew by compass and ground speed indicator. The fog below them cleared just enough for them to spot Folkestone and the south coast as they crossed it, but they were unable to keep their promise to fly low over the Borton family garden at Yalding in Kent and see the message 'GODSPEED' that Biffy had whitewashed in the field beside the house in letters fifteen feet high.[1] They were right on course and their spirits were high. Ross Smith described the scene in his diary:

> The machine was flying stately as a rock. All the bracing wires were tuned to a nicety. The dope on the huge planes glinted and glistened in the sunlight. I was filled with admiration. The engines, which were throttled down to about three quarters of their possible speed, had settled down to their task and were purring away in perfect unison and harmony. When both engines are going well and synchronised to the same speed, the roar of the exhausts develops into one long sustained rhythmical boom-boom-boom. It is a song of pleasant harmony to the pilot, a duet of contentment that sings of perfect firing in both engines and says that all is well.

This, of course, echoes the impression recorded by T.E. Lawrence about his flight from Paris in a Handley Page six months before.

Paris was not a refuelling point on this flight. Because they were in a Vimy and not a Handley Page, they could easily reach Lyon in one hop. Over the French coast they encountered thick cloud. First they tried flying below it but found this impossible because of snow. So they climbed and climbed and eventually came out of the cloud into bright dazzling sunshine at 9,000 feet, which was getting near their limit, given the loss of power that occurs with altitude and the heavy load of petrol on board. Ross Smith wrote the following account in the *National Geographic Magazine*, published in March 1921.

> We were then just above the clouds. Below us the storm raged, but we had entered another world – a strange world all of our own, with bright dazzling sunshine. It might have been a

vision of the polar regions – it undoubtedly felt like it ... The rounded cloud contours might have been the domes of snow covered summits. It was hard to believe that the amorphous expanse was not solid. Here and there flocculent towers and ramps heaved up, piled like mighty snow dumps, toppling and crashing into one another. Everything was so tremendous, so vast.

Below, the shadow of our machine pursued us, skipping from crest to crest, jumping gulfs and ridges like a bewitched phantom. My brother worked out our course and I headed the machine on to the compass bearing for Lyon. On we went, riding the silver edged sea and chased by our dancing shadow ... The cold grew more intense. Our hands and feet lost all feeling and our bodies became well-nigh frozen. The icy wind penetrated our thick clothing and it was with the greatest difficulty that I could work on the machine. Our breath condensed on our faces and face-masks and iced up our goggles and helmets.

Occasionally immense cloud barriers faced us and there was no circumventing them. They were invariably charged with snow and as I plunged the machine into them, the wings and fuselage were quickly armoured with ice. Our air speed indicator became choked white with an accumulating layer of driving snow. Goggles were useless owing to the ice and we suffered much agony through being compelled to keep a look-out with unprotected eyes, straining into the 90 mile an hour snow blast.

About 1pm I suggested to my brother that we should have some sandwiches for lunch. On taking them from the cupboard we discovered that they were frozen hard. Fortunately we carried a thermos of hot coffee and the pieces de resistance were a few sticks of chocolate which were part of our emergency rations. I have never felt so cold and miserable in my whole life.

The Vimy and its crew flew on for three hours by dead reckoning. They had to keep above the clouds. To descend into them for any length of time would have weighed them down with an unsupportable coating of ice. Then Providence came to their rescue. In front of them a cloud-free funnel, 7,000 feet deep, appeared, down which they corkscrewed to 1,000 feet, and identified

Roanne – only 40 miles from their destination. They landed easily at Marseille after a 500-mile flight, which Smith said later was the worst stage of the whole journey.

They were delayed in leaving next morning, because of difficulty in finding hot water to refill their radiators, which had been drained the night before as a precaution against frost. They got off at 10 o'clock and flew, with the landscape spread out clearly below them, towards their next destination, Rome. They flew low over Monte Carlo and Nice and could see crowds watching them from the Promenade des Anglais. They thought of landing for a day in the Casino but decided against it because it was the 13th.

Like most of the RAF pilots on the route before them, they encountered strong headwinds over northern Italy. With T.E. Lawrence's and the Darley brothers' experience in mind, they abandoned Rome as their target and landed instead at the Pisa route station. The OC of the route station was Captain Horn who took them to a hotel in Pisa for the night. There was heavy rain and in the morning, when Smith tried to taxi the machine into position for a take-off, it sank into the mud.

The story now switches to another source of information. As the flight progressed, Ross Smith telegraphed daily reports back to Vickers at Weybridge and Vickers relayed these to *The Times*. Here is an edited version of the report for 16 November.

> We had heavy rain at Pisa and the plane became bogged down. We had to use planks under the wheels and lots of Italian mechanics to get the machine ready to move. Bennett remained on the ground while we started the engines and held the tail down until the machine was moving. Then he made a running jump at the rear cockpit and was hauled aboard by Shiers as the machine was leaving the ground. The aerodrome was two inches under water but the Vimy rose beautifully into the air and we landed at Rome at about three o'clock.

Anyone who has looked at the Vimy in the RAF Museum will agree that the leap to the cockpit, which Bennett made, was athletic. The rim of the cockpit into which he had to scramble, with Shiers' help, is about eight feet off the ground and there are control wires running down the side of the fuselage, which must not be interfered with. They must have shared the rear cockpit for the next leg of the journey since the two pilots were in the way of a crawl through to the nose to use the other seat.

November 17th

Left Rome yesterday morning 9am. Low cloud and bad visibility. Passed over Capua and Naples then turned east over mountains and flew low over Vesuvius but weather too bad for photography. Very bumpy over mountains, machine falling several hundred feet at times but good wind helping us. Arrived Taranto at 11.45. Suda Bay reported good so decided to land there to avoid the long sea stretch. Left Taranto at 8am. Strong wind on our beam with low clouds and rain all the way to south Greece. Attempted to get above clouds but they were too high so flew at 800 feet. Following the coast we very nearly hit a small mountainous island in the mist. From south Greece to Crete good weather, arrived Suda 3.45pm. Aerial route station here giving every assistance. Hope Cairo tomorrow. Crew fit. Hoping for better weather now. Much warmer.

The account in the *National Geographic Magazine* has a little more to say about their brief stopover in Crete:

After a good night's rest in comfortable beds, we were up at our usual hour and made an early start for Suda Bay. Once again the weather was cruel to us. Low cloud and rain forced us down to no more than 800 feet. First we flew east to the heel of Italy and then headed across the open sea to the island of Corfu. Almost before we realised it, Corfu loomed up in the mist and I altered course to the south east and flew down the coast of Greece. The bad weather made our voyage down this rugged coast very hazardous and on one occasion after passing through a particularly low bank of cloud, I was terrified to observe a rocky island looming up in the mist directly ahead. It was only by turning sharply at right angles that I avoided crashing the machine against its precipitous sides. All this time we were flying at no more than 800 feet and so it was with intense relief that we reached Cape

Matea, the most southerly point of Greece and headed across the open sea to Crete.

The clouds were now lifted and the mists dissipated, unfolding a scene of rare enchantment. The high ranges of Crete soon loomed up before us. A layer of cloud encircled the island like a great wreath. The mountains rose nobly above it and the coasts, rocky and surfbeaten, could be seen below us. All this set in a sea of wondrous blue, bathed in bright sunshine. It was a gladsome and welcome sight.

Wheeling above the town of Chania, which is on the opposite side of a narrow neck to Suda Bay, we soon located the aerodrome and circled above it preparatory to landing. The aerodrome is not of the best and is rather a tricky place for negotiating a landing, being surrounded on three sides by high, rocky hills, but we succeeded in making a good landing. Here too we were welcomed by an officer of the Royal Air Force[2] and a small crowd of inhabitants who gathered round the machine, examining it and us with curious interest.

With the knowledge that on the morrow our longest oversea flight in this half of the voyage awaited us, we spent most of the

The town of Chania in 1919. It is now ten times larger. (Air2/83/B4735)

206

afternoon on a particularly thorough overhaul of the machine and then accepted our RAF friend's invitation to look over the town and take tea at his house. We found Canea [Chania] to be an extremely picturesque and interesting old place. Its massive castle walls, its narrow cobbled streets and its quaint, old fashioned but substantial buildings, reminiscent of a bygone age, are all in keeping with its history which runs back to the beginning of the Christian era and several leagues before that. Our pilot excited our admiration by the expert way in which he steered us through a maze of rough surfaced alleys in his Ford, causing a great scattering of children and dogs – both of which appear to thrive here in large numbers.[3]

Eventually he conducted us to a quaint little cafe – a sort of tavern at which people seem to forgather by custom for a cup of coffee before dinner. The *cafe au lait* was excellent and, as our host racily recounted his experiences, I came to the conclusion that life in Canea, small and isolated though it is, holds compensations and is not nearly so dull as it appears at first glance.[4]

Rough surfaced alleys in Chania in 1919. Children in the street in Chania 1919. A donkey carrying brushwood is blocking the road. (LGS)

The open-topped Ford Tourer in which Lewis or Semple gave the Australians a tour of Chania. My father took this photo in Venizelos Square in the summer of 1919, not long before the Australians arrived. (LGS)

Just before they set off from Suda Bay they received a telegram from their Prime Minister Billy Hughes:

> Do your best, but do nothing foolhardy. If you cannot make Australia within 30 days, never mind. Good luck.

Chanian Muslims relaxing on the waterfront in the late summer of 1919. They look contented but they would all be expelled to Turkey in 1923. In their place would come 20,000 Orthodox Christians expelled from Anatolia. (LGS)

The tomb of a Turkish general on the outskirts of Chania in 1919. It was on the route that the Australians travelled from Suda into Chania on 17 November 1919. (LGS)

In 2000 the Turkish General's tomb was still there but it had become a kebab take-away. There is little respect between Orthodox Christian Cretans and Muslim Turks as I discovered during talks with the staff in the Chania Tourist Office. (CS)

Reading between the lines Hughes has realized that the stipulation that the flight must be completed in 30 days was inappropriate. If the machine and its crew reached Australia at all it would be magnificent and would deserve the £10,000 prize.

There is another account of the flight in Nelson Eustis' book, *The England to Australia Air Race*, which continues the story:

> The 650 miles to Cairo included 450 over the sea before they would sight the African port of Sollum.[5] Although the Rolls Royce engines were performing to perfection, the crew took the precaution to inflate four inner tubes, the usual life rafts in those days. One faulty magneto was replaced.
>
> An early departure had been arranged but as usual rain was falling. The high mountain tops were shrouded in clouds making navigation difficult. The RAF officer suggested that there existed a somewhat narrow passage through the mountains. It was his opinion that this might be free of clouds. The only aid to navigation, in the absence of helpful railway lines, was a rough goat track leading to the pass. Worried that the aerodrome might become boggy with the continual rain, Ross Smith decided to leave immediately Bennett and Shiers gave their OK to the engines. They were airborne at 8.12am, a decision having been made to try their luck with the mountain passage. The choice was a good one although the flying was not easy. The clouds were low but there was just enough space for the Vimy. It seemed to the crew that the aircraft cleared the jagged mountains by only a few feet, not only below but on port and starboard as well.

'As usual rain was falling' is misleading. The rain that was falling that morning was almost the first that Suda had seen for three months but Ross Smith knew that because of the absence of drainage, the airfield would soon become waterlogged. That is why they took off so quickly. Given the terrain, the absence of railways was inevitable. But in 1919, there were no roads across the island either. There were just goat tracks, which were also used by men, donkeys and mules. The pass through the mountains was no problem given good visibility. There was low cloud and they had to fly almost within the mountain pass. It was worth it. Flying right round the western end of the island or flying east to

Heraklion before turning south, would have added ninety miles to the journey and used up an hour's petrol.

The pass that they used was the one that a Handley Page pilot, Flight Lieutenant Higgs, had found earlier in the summer. At its southern end is the Imbros Gorge and not the better known Samaria Gorge, the approach to which is too steep for a climbing aircraft. The approach to the Imbros Gorge from the east end of Suda Bay is gradual and this would have given the Vimy the twenty minutes needed to reach the necessary four or five thousand feet while making good headway south. It was not the Gorge itself that was helpful. It is much too narrow to fly in. What mattered was the long gradual approach to this low point (1,181 metres) in the mountainous spine of the island. See colour photos.

The over-sea flight to the African coast was about 300 miles, which does not seem very much until one realizes that with a cruising speed of between 50 and 60 knots and petrol for eight hours flying, headwinds could use up petrol at an alarming rate. No petrol could be spared for half an hour spent climbing in circles over Suda Bay. The gradual nature of the curving climb up to the Askifou Plateau can be seen from the colour photograph, which was taken about one third of the way across the island. Suda Bay is round to the right behind the hill in the right foreground. The White Mountains are to the west and Mount Ida is to the east, behind the camera. Both reach up to 7,600 feet. Clouds form as hot air from Africa is forced up by the mountain crest and the Vimy had to keep below them, which was just possible in the gap at Imbros. The goat track that the Vimy followed is there but alongside now runs a tarmac road with hairpin bends up to Askifou and down again to the south coast at Hora Sfakion. See colour photo.

There was still no road in 1941 and the allied troops retreating to Hora Sfakion in May had to make do with the goat track. They were terribly exposed to German dive bombers until they reached the safety of the narrow Imbros Gorge where they lay low until nightfall and the Navy came to take them off. Evelyn Waugh was one of them.

In my father's collection there is a photograph of the Vimy, with the crew standing in front of it. Ross Smith was grateful for help at the airfield and advice about the route. The photo bears the signatures of all the crew and was taken on the airfield at

Ross and Keith Smith's Vickers Vimy at Hounslow before take-off on 12 November 1919. Ross Smith gave this signed print to my father as a thank you for hospitality and advice about the route across Crete.

Another photograph given to my father. From left to right: Bennett, Keith Smith, Ross Smith, Shiers.

Hounslow before the departure. They must have taken a stock of these signed photos with them in the plane to hand out to anyone who did them a good turn. They also gave my father a close-up photograph of the crew.

The souvenir collecting did not end there. Leslie frequently mentions in his 1918 diary his sister Doris who married Billy Vidler, a Queensland soldier, just before the end of the war. Billy's home was in Townsville and as soon as the war was over Billy and Doris sailed on a troopship for Australia, arriving sometime in the first half of 1919. The Vimy only stayed overnight at Suda but before it took off next morning Leslie had written two identical letters to his sister, which he gave to Ross Smith. The Vimy was carrying 'first day covers' from England for philatelists and also a special cancellation stamp marked 'Per Vickers Vimy Aeroplane to Australia', which Ross Smith applied to my father's envelopes before he took off. One of these two letters has survived and is now in my possession. It is to be donated to the Australian War Memorial museum. See colour photo.

> Per Aerial Mail "I" Station,
> Vickers Vimy No. 1 Aerial Route,
> London to Australia Race Suda Bay, Crete.
>
> November 1919
>
> My dear Doris,
>
> I am sending this letter along with another by the first machine to fly from London to Australia in the big race for £10,000. The machine landed here yesterday and we filled it up and executed a minor repair. They expect to leave this morning in spite of very bad weather.
>
> I do not expect to leave here yet and am having quite a good time. These fellows brought the news along that a Committee of Enquiry is being held in England on No. 1 Aerial Route – which is now known as the Trail of Death – owing to the accidents on it. Cheerful what! No more now.
>
> Love to all.
Your affect. brother Les.
>
> P.S. Will you please return this letter to me as I should like it as a souvenir. I have sent another to you in the same way.

The letter is written in pencil and very faded. On the back of the letter he has written:

> Per Vickers Vimy – markings G.EA.OU competitor in London to Australia Race for £10,000. First m/c to land at Suda bay on its way.
>
> Pilots Capt. Smith MC DFC, AFC and Lt. Smith

According to Semple, the markings G.EA.OU were interpreted by the crew as 'God 'Elp All Of Us'.

Now we return to Ross Smith's report to Vickers for 18 November, which, like the others, appeared in *The Times* next day:

> Left Suda Bay at eight today. Weather again bad. Low cloud made crossing Crete mountains difficult. Had to fly at 2,000 feet through rain most of the way across the Med. Passed two steamers and checked ground speed and drift on them. Crossing took two and a half hours. Struck African coast at Sollum then flew east to Cairo across desert via Matruh and Wadi Natrum. Hope for Damascus and Baghdad tomorrow. Hope for better weather now. So far we have taken 30 flying hours – mostly through rain and storms.
>
> Throughout the greatest assistance rendered by aerial route stations, nothing being too much trouble. It is largely due to their excellent organisation that we are here so soon. Vimy going perfectly.

Ross Smith has here gone out of his way to show his appreciation of the staff on the aerial route. Since he did not leave England until 12 November he must have been well aware of the adverse criticism of No. 1 Aerial Route that had circulated in the newspapers and in Parliament since 1 November. Indeed, it would have been wise of him to study it closely. His comments were opportune and, when they appeared in *The Times*, may well have influenced the Committee of Enquiry in its findings. Like the route pioneer Borton, Ross Smith was carrying his own spares and his two travelling mechanics were proven, self sufficient experts. When they loaded up the plane at Hounslow they found that they were 300 lb overweight. Smith refused to discard a single spare so they jettisoned all their personal belongings except their toothbrushes.

* * *

At this point it is convenient to follow the paths of the remaining competitors in the race and we will return to the flight of Ross Smith and his crew in the Vimy when the fate of everyone else has been determined.

* * *

On 21 November, Val Rendle took off from Hounslow in the Blackburn Kangaroo. The aircraft's registration letters were G-EAOW which they interpreted as 'England-Australia On Wings'. They were the first to enter the race after the rules were published but had long delays because it was decided to upgrade their Rolls-Royce engines from 250 to 275hp – still a lot less than the 360hp of the Vimy that Ross Smith had been given through Borton's influence. Rendle followed No. 1 Aerial Route but encountered dreadful weather all the way.

> Telegram Taranto to Air Ministry. 28 November.
>
> Please report movements of Kangaroo to RAF Malta. Present location of this machine, if known will assist in planning close down of Taranto. I am not delaying close down of other stations in Italy on account of Australian machines. Please wire if you agree.

> Telegram Air Ministry to Taranto. 28 November.
>
> Present location of Kangaroo not known as pilot altering original plans. Kangaroo proceeds via Malta. Not due to touch Taranto. Proceed with closing down of route stations but give Australian competitors available assistance on demand.

On the same day that Taranto was trying to find out where the Kangaroo was, it landed at St Raphael having left Lyon on 26 November. The Smith brothers in the Vickers Vimy were by this time at Calcutta.

215

The Blackburn Kangaroo taking off from Hounslow on 21 November 1919. The angle of climb for such a low powered machine seems extraordinary. (Q114553)

Back in England, on 4 December, Howell and Fraser took off in their Martinsyde A1 and followed No. 1 Aerial Route as far as Taranto, which they reached on 8 December. They spent the night at the RAF station and took off again for Greece next morning. The plane was seen at dusk over Corfu. They had apparently been flying for eight hours in misty weather but had only covered 150 miles, suggesting that they were lost. Minutes later the machine came down in St George's Bay – probably out of fuel. Local people, interviewed later, said that cries for help were heard but the sea was too rough for assistance to be given. The plane was later found in twelve feet of water and Captain Howell's body was washed ashore. Fraser's body was never found. A steward at the Taranto Route Station found Howell's wallet in his bedroom, after they had taken off, and had to ask for details of his next of kin from the Air Ministry so that he could post it to them.

Mystery still surrounds this flight. Is it possible that, just short of Valona, Howell realized he had left his wallet behind and turned back to collect it? That would explain how they had flown for so long but apparently covered such a short distance. Captain Howell's father, in Australia, put forward a theory that they had landed safely on Corfu, then been killed and robbed and the plane and their bodies pushed into the sea. The theory was never substantiated and nothing came of it.

Howell's wife, whom he had met and married while in England, was on board the *Orsova*, en route to Australia to meet him. Howell had intended to overtake the liner off shore near Naples where he planned to circle round it. When news of the accident came through on the ship's radio, no one could bear to tell her what had happened. She did not find out until the ship reached Adelaide where Howell's father was waiting to break the news. Captain Howell's body was later exhumed at Corfu and brought to his home town of Heidelberg in Victoria, where he was buried with full military honours. He was a flying ace on the Western Front who had been awarded the MC, DFC and the DSO.

Parer and MacIntosh in the DH9 were the last crew in the race to follow No. 1 Aerial Route and they dropped a wreath in St George's Bay Corfu, on 13 February 1920 as they passed over en route to Athens. They were not the winners of the race but they did eventually reach Australia. Despite being out of the race, they were, in fact, the second crew to reach Australia from England by air and the first to fly to Australia in a single-engined machine. They reached Suda Bay on 18 February 1920 and Australia on 2 August. Eustis Nelson described their flight as 'a triumph over adversity'.

The Kangaroo evidently did not take the Malta route and after delays caused by fog, the mistral, gales, and malicious damage,

Parer and MacIntosh's DH9 in the Australian War Memorial Museum at Canberra.

finally made it to Taranto, across to Greece and onward to Crete, where it landed on 5 December. Presumably, Suda reported this to Taranto who relayed the news to the Air Ministry. By now the rains had come and flooded the airfield at Suda. It will be remembered that when Lieutenant Halliday prepared the airfield in a great hurry, before General Borton's flight the previous summer, he had simply filled in all the drainage ditches in order to get a long enough landing strip. He then rolled it flat with the steam roller lent to him by the governor of the island.

The Blackburn Kangaroo made a smooth landing but sank in the mud up to its axles just as the Vimy had at Pisa. Semple had seen all this before at Bleharies on the Belgian border almost a year previously when he had rescued a Handley Page from a muddy turnip field. Once again he collected stacks of timber on to which the machine was hauled after being dug out of the mud.

There was no shortage of labour. The Greeks had a camp of unrepatriated Bulgarian prisoners of war on the island. They lived inside the old Turkish arsenal in a building that Leslie photographed. This is now an office block in the Greek naval station where the discussions with Mr Potamitakis took place during research for this book. That prisoners of war should still be there a year after the war had ended seems strange and it may be that

The Kangaroo being dug out of the mud. (LGS)

The Kangaroo being hauled up onto planks by the Bulgarian prisoners of war. (LGS)

many of them hoped to stay in Crete. Well to the west of Chania there is a village called Voulgharo, which is Greek for 'Bulgarians'. It might also be so named because of the many exchanges of Christian and Muslim populations that took place in the 1920s under the auspices of the League of Nations. If the prisoners of war were Muslim they would not have been allowed to remain after 1923.

There was no shortage of labour. (LGS)

Leslie Semple with Valdemar Rendle, the senior pilot. Semple looks tactlessly cheerful. (LGS)

It took three days to get everything ready for the Blackburn Kangaroo's departure. From the next photograph it looks as though Leslie enjoyed the task rather more than Valdemar Rendle who was the principal pilot.

The Kangaroo took off on the morning of 8 December heading for North Africa and Semple duly reported this to Taranto.

> Telegram Taranto to Air Ministry. 9th December.
>
> Kangaroo left Suda for Sollum on the 8th. Suda Bay now very boggy. Closing down station fast.

The report was premature. Before the Kangaroo had been in the air for more than an hour an oil pipe broke and Rendle had to turn round and head for the Suda airfield again on one engine. At the last minute, to aid the landing, as he thought, he switched on the other engine which, being without oil, promptly seized up. With only one engine and the airfield mostly under water, he did not make a good landing. The plane overshot and tipped up

The sad end of the flight of the Kangaroo – 8 December 1919. (LGS)

on its nose in a ditch. Nobody was hurt and the machine was not badly damaged but they were not carrying spares for this kind of damage and these would have to come from London. Rendle made plans to return to London to get them and fly back

The site of the Suda airfield in 2000. The photo was taken standing on the hillside behind the Kangaroo in the previous picture. The ditch left centre is where the Kangaroo ended its journey. (CS)

221

to Crete but before he could do so news came through that the Vimy had reached Darwin on 10 December and claimed the £10,000 prize.

The Kangaroo attempt was abandoned but the luckless mechanic, Lieutenant Potts, was left behind to look after the plane. He was still there when the very belated, but ultimately successful, DH9 of Parer and McIntosh arrived on 18 February 1920. Parer and McIntosh may well have been the last to use this undrained quagmire. By World War Two a new and dry airfield had been constructed at Maleme, a few miles west of Chania, which was a great help to the German troop-carrying gliders and Junkers JU52s when they arrived in 1941.

The Director of Training and Organization reported to the Chief of the Air Staff on 8 January 1920 that the Suda Bay base had indeed been handed over to the Greeks.

Lieutenant Semple left Suda Bay for good on 27 December. He managed to arrange his return journey to England with a stop-over in Athens instead of Constantinople. His album shows that he saw the temples of the Acropolis and the ancient stadium below it. He went by ship from Athens to Brindisi and then by train to London, arriving on 12 January. He was demobilized on 20 January and the next day his airmail letter arrived at his sister's home in Townsville.

He had just one more duty to perform before he began his new life in London. See the next photo.

Whether the Blackburn Aero Co. succeeded in its insurance claim is not revealed. The surprising thing is that an insurance company had been willing to take on the risk on *any* terms after all that had gone before. On the basis of the No. 1 Aerial Route experience a premium of 33 per cent of the sum insured would have been needed just to provide cover as far as Cairo, and Cairo was less than a quarter of the way to Australia.

Of the seven machines that took part in the official race to Australia, three were written off when they crashed, two were written off later, and two made it to Australia. Four of the eighteen airmen taking part were killed. The Caudron IV that got as far as Rangoon was also written off. That is only what Air Vice Marshal Ellington would have expected. This was pioneer flying.

* * *

A letter that Leslie Semple received soon after his return to England. It was written by the pilot of the Blackburn Kangaroo who was trying to claim on his insurance policy for the crash at Chania.

Now we can return to describe the remainder of the victorious flight of the Vickers Vimy.

* * *

On 19 November the the Vimy took off from Cairo for Damascus, following the route that Ross Smith had taken with Generals

223

Borton and Salmond the year before. The route over Romani, El Arish, Gaza and Nazareth was familiar to Ross Smith. When still in the army and in charge of a machine gun battery, he had taken part in the Battle of Romani and later this was where he had most of his dogfights with German and Turkish pilots when he was a pilot in No. 1 Squadron of the Australian Flying Corps.

The next day they reached Baghdad where they were looked after by the 10th Indian Lancers. While there a 'simoon' blew up. This is a hot, dry and dusty gale only to be found in the Sahara and Arabian deserts. The machine was lashed down and the Indian Lancers clung on to it all through the night. The next day they had to dig out the machine from the sand and in the afternoon flew on to Basra, passing over Kut-el-Amarah where General Townshend and his army had surrendered to the Turks in 1916.

On 24 November the Australians reached Karachi, the next day Delhi and Calcutta on the 28th. The flying was as trouble free as it had been the previous year when Ross Smith had been flying with Borton. The Vickers Vimy overtook Poulet at Akyab in Burma on 29 November. This was not surprising since Poulet's twin-engined Caudron had engines with less than a quarter of the horsepower of the Vimy and there were mountains in the way. Here is Ross Smith's own account of his meeting with Poulet, taken from the Angus & Robertson book on the expedition:

> We were of course not alone in the race. The gallant Frenchman Poulet had a twenty-eight days start. His handicap was a machine totally unsuited to the enterprise. It was not till we reached Karachi in India on the 24th of November that we had news of him; thence in a series of day stages, Delhi, Allahabad, Calcutta, we had the excitement of his progress, and the satisfaction of finding that we were catching up. On approaching Akyab in Burma, we noticed another machine at an aerodrome. It turned out to be Poulet's. In the flight from Akyab to Rangoon, Poulet was also in the air and reached the city shortly after we did. We greatly admired his pluck in tackling the huge job in a small machine accompanied by a single mechanic. The gallant Frenchman received with us the hospitality of His Excellency Sir Reginald Craddock, the Lieutenant Governor of Burma and Lady Craddock at

Rangoon. Monsieur Poulet had made a daring and glorious endeavour. Great honour and credit are due to him, but after leaving Rangoon we, in our modern Vickers Vimy, left him behind.

The rest of the journey is best described in Ross Smith's own words:

> We had intended to fly direct from Bangkok to Singapore, but as we were informed that there was a good aerodrome at Singora, about half-way, we decided to halt there. The Siamese notion of a good aerodrome nearly brought us all to an untimely end. A square patch had been hewn from the jungle, the trunks and upper portions of the trees had been removed but the stumps were allowed to remain. We made a safe and miraculous landing, missing the stumps by inches. The 3rd December, the heaviest rain I have ever experienced, kept us tied up at Singora, and Sergeant Bennett was busy repairing the tail skid which had found one of the obstacles on the Singora aerodrome. He worked all day on it using a lathe at a local rice mill which was turned round by coolies. They went on strike and we had to beat them and bribe them to get the job finished by dark.

The Caudron G4. It weighed less than half a Vimy and its engines had only 100hp each. (Q58494)

It rained hard all day and the machine stood on an island surrounded by six inches to a foot of water. We were wet through and had no dry clothes to put on but none of us got fever fortunately.

I approached the local governor and secured twenty convicts to clear a track through the stumps on the aerodrome for getting off. The petrol arrived about dark but it was raining too hard for us to put it into the machine that night.

From Penang onwards there was very little rain and we flew along at 1,500 feet under the clouds. We passed over several cleared patches but there appeared to be no natural landing grounds anywhere. Any country that is flat is usually swampy or paddy land while the higher ground is timbered.

On the 4th December, my birthday, we arrived at Singapore. The racecourse had been prepared for us to land upon and proved very suitable although too small with houses all round it. I made a slow landing and just before we touched down Sergeant Bennett slid along the top of the fuselage down to the tail and the machine pulled up in about 80 yards. This was Bennett's own idea and it is a very useful thing to remember when landing on a small ground.

That night we were entertained by the Australian and New Zealand Association of Malaya. Next day, the 5th we left Singapore for Kalidjati near Batavia in Java. This was a distance of nearly 700 miles and the worst stage of the journey as regards landing grounds. We travelled 200 miles down the eastern coast of Sumatra, which was so densely wooded that it would have been impossible to have made a forced landing. Then we turned seawards to Batavia. The machine was not climbing so well now and took longer to get off the ground. This was due to the different atmosphere and the fact that the fabric was becoming slacker from the dew and the rain of the night before. After the sun became hot the fabric would become normal again.

We arrived at Kalidjati where we were received by the Governor-General of the Dutch East Indies. We had expected that the last stage of the journey, from Singapore to Darwin would be the most difficult. But the Governor-General, on hearing that aeroplanes were flying from England to Australia, ordered aerodromes to be constructed at different points in the Dutch Islands. These greatly facilitated our flight. On 6th December we arrived at Soerabaya after passing over most glorious scenery but we found that the aerodrome had been placed on reclaimed land, so that on landing our machine became deeply bogged.

The thirty days of the competition were now closing in and anxieties increased. We extricated the machine with the greatest difficulty and at one time I feared that it would be impossible ever to start off from that aerodrome again. I had a roadway of bamboo mats laid down 350 yards long and 40 yards wide. The machine was hauled from the bog by a horde of natives to this improvised pathway. We made a perilous take-off with bamboo flying in all directions and late in the afternoon of the 8th of December we landed at Bima in Soembawa. On the 9th of December we left Bima for Atamboea in Timor and flew east along the north coast of Flores and the south east to Timor. We were very glad to land safely in Timor as it meant only 350 miles from there to Darwin.

Tired as we were, excitement kept us all from sleep that night. All going well we should land in Australia on the

The Vimy over the Dutch East Indies – 6 December 1919. (NASM 00175734)

morrow. Before daybreak on the 10th we were down at the machine giving it the last test and overhaul before venturing on the wide stretch of sea. At 8.35am we taxied into a light breeze and took off with beautiful weather in our favour. As our hours rolled slowly by we strained our eyes towards Australia. A tiny speck upon the waters resolved itself into a warship, H.M.A.S. *Sydney* in exactly the position we had asked her to be in case of need. The clouds and mist obscured all distant vision and it was not until after 3 o'clock that I observed the first faint outline of land. The land speedily assumed more definite contour and details became manifest. Darwin came into view. In a few minutes we were circling above the town. Then down, down in a steep descending spiral – and we had touched Australian soil![6]

Darwin was the official completion of the journey. It had taken 28 days of which the flying time was 135 hours and the distance covered 11,340 miles at an average speed of 84mph. On landing on Darwin racecourse they were treated to a number of welcoming speeches.[7] The speech delivered by the Mayor of Darwin was in flowery prose and it was an emotional occasion:

The citizens of the Northern Territory of Australia are privileged to be the first to welcome you valiant knights of the air, who have crossed the wide continents and oceans of the world, whose dauntless courage has conquered the last of the elements, and made it the handmaid of progress and civilisation. We are especially gratified to feel that the victory has been won by Australians, who have been trained in many an aerial conflict in the late war. This great contest over space, in which you have been so signally successful, has placed the coping stone on the triumphal arch raised by ability and Australian valor on the great battle fields of the world. It has enshrined Australian chivalry and resource in the Pantheon of the nations, where the whole world will do homage to your unique exploit.

That same evening Billie Hughes made a speech at Castlemaine near Melbourne:

CASTLEMAINE. When Mr. Hughes announced the arrival of Captain Ross Smith at Darwin at his meeting at Castlemaine on Wednesday night there was a great outburst of enthusiasm, the audience cheering for several minutes. Mr. Hughes said:

'This is an epoch in the history of Australia and aviation. Although you may not realise it, we have this day overcome, as it were, those geographical disabilities that hedge us about. It has now been proved possible, with that organisation which can be created for us, to reach Europe in from 12 to 15 days. We have proved once more that in this, as in all other things, Australia is in the forefront. It is a great thing that an Australian has been the first to get here, and that he has beaten all comers easily. What did he do it for? Not for the £10,000, for the little he would get out of it he could put in his eye. He has done it for the honor of Australia.'

It was at Darwin that the Smith brothers were notified of their knighthoods and Shiers and Bennett were awarded bars to their

The arrival at Darwin – 10 December 1919. (National Archives of Australia, (L84857)

Air Force Medals. Public opinion in Australia rightly objected to the differentiation in honours between the officers and the mechanics – Shiers and Bennett – whose contribution in skill and hard work, must have been every bit as great as that of Keith Smith. The decision to knight the two officers but not the mechanics was probably made by King George V or his entourage. Considering Billy Hughes' character it is unlikely to have been made by him. Shiers and Bennett were later awarded honorary commissions in the Australian Flying Corps.

From Darwin the Australian Government had organized an overland route of 2,396 miles to Melbourne with a further eleven refuelling points. So the plane flew on to Brisbane, where Ross Smith posted the letters for Leslie's sister Doris, who lived at Townsville. See colour photo. The envelopes were given a penny ha'penny stamp when they reached Brisbane and these were franked at 7 p.m. on 7 January 1920. They then travelled by land mail north to Townsville where they arrived on 21 January. The official bag of airmail sent by philatelists was not handed over to the Prime Minister in Melbourne until five weeks later.

But my father's letter didn't receive the commemorative stamp and postmark that were applied to the letters in the mail bag that Ross Smith handed to the Prime Minister later in Melbourne.

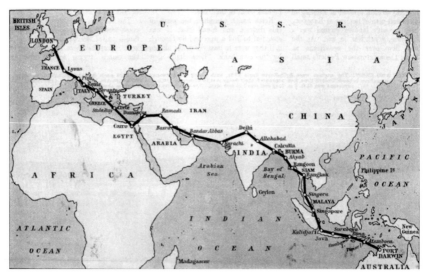

The map shows how closely they hugged the land all the way from Bangkok to Darwin.

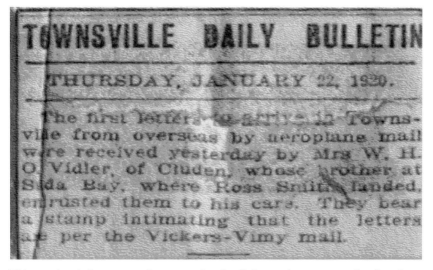

This cutting is important. It proves that Leslie's two letters were the first from Europe to be delivered in Australia and that they bore the Vickers Vimy over-stamp applied by Ross Smith.

The Vimy flew on to Sydney, which it reached on 14 February. It arrived in Melbourne on 25 February and on 27 February Prime Minister Billy Hughes received the bag of specially franked letters from England and handed over the cheque for £10,000. The whole flight involved fifty-five landings.

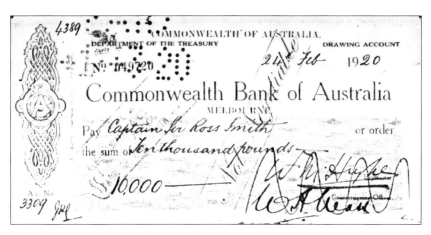

The cheque that Billy Hughes handed to Ross Smith. The proceeds were divided equally between the four members of the crew.

During the welcome celebrations Billy Hughes made a speech that included the following:

> This latest and greatest development of the possibilities of aerial navigation has not only been conceived and organised by Australians, but has also been consummated by Australians.

Brigadier Borton was not mentioned, which says much for the Australian psyche at the time. His experience, skill and influence had played a major part in the success of the flight. He had flown the whole route from England to Calcutta and, with Ross Smith beside him, reconnoitered it to within 350 miles of Australia. It was his influence that enabled the Smith brothers to obtain the Vimy from Vickers and he explained the details of the route to the participating crews. None of those who took part in the competition had done so much.

Before taking a jaundiced view of the lack of recognition for Borton's role in the project we should remember that Australia was a young country and in need of heroes of its own. After the huge voluntary efforts that Australians had made on behalf of the Allies in France, in Egypt and at Gallipoli, Australia surely deserved some.[8]

We should not be too hard on Sir Ross Smith either. Borton may have failed to win a knighthood but he married Muriel Slater, a young divorcee whom he met in Simla in 1923. He was thirty-seven and this gave him a readymade family and an energetic wife who looked after him for the rest of his life. He remained in the RAF and rose to be an air vice marshal. He commuted in a private aeroplane from Kent to the Air Ministry where he was Director of Personnel Services, until he retired in 1933. He then enjoyed another thirty-three years as a well respected and still monocled country gentleman, who always had an eye for a pretty girl.[9]

Ross Smith was not so fortunate. Like Sir John Alcock who was the first to fly the Atlantic, Sir Ross Smith paid the typical price for his daring. On 13 April 1922 he took off from Brooklands, Weybridge, in a Vickers Vulture amphibian, which he was planning to use in a round the world flight. His brother Keith, who should have been in the plane with him, arrived at Brooklands

Sir Keith MacPherson Smith KBE.

Sir Ross MacPherson Smith KBE MC DFC AFC.

late. He was on the ground watching and saw the machine slip into a low altitude spin and crash. Ross and his faithful mechanic Bennett were killed instantly. Sir Keith Smith, on the other hand, became a director of Quantas Airways and lived until 1955.

My Aunt Doris gave birth to a son soon after Ross Smith died. She called her son Keith. Four years later my brother was born. He was also called Keith. But for the crash at Weybridge in 1922, presumably they would both have been called Ross. The Australian all-round cricketer, Keith Miller, famous in Test series after World War Two, was born during their epic flight. His full name is Keith Ross Miller.

After all the ceremonies were over in Melbourne the Vickers Vimy flew on to the Smith brothers' and Shiers' home town of Adelaide where it rests until this day in a special showcase near the airport terminal. See colour photos. Alcock and Brown's Vimy, which flew the Atlantic, hangs in the Science Museum in Kensington and there is a third Vimy in the RAF Museum at Hendon. A replica Vimy flew the route from London to Melbourne in 1994. No Handley Page O/100s, O/400s or V/1500s survive despite the fact that more than five hundred were built in Britain

The Smith brothers' original Vickers Vimy in its showcase in Adelaide.
(Optical Design)

The showcase at Adelaide West Beach Airport where the Vimy is now housed.
(Optical Design)

and a hundred more were in production in the USA at the time of the armistice. Perhaps a film maker will pick up this story and build one.

Notes

1. Personal communication with Borton's step-grandson, Guy Slater.
2. Captain Lewis or Lieutenant Semple. Ross Smith's account mentions only one RAF officer.
3. This sounds like my father but we have no proof. He was just twenty years old.
4. 'Racily recounting his experiences' also sounds like my father.
5. The oversea distance is in fact only 300 miles. Borton made it more because he flew east to Heraklion first.
6. Sir Ross Smith – *The First Aeroplane Voyage from England to Australia*. Angus & Robertson Ltd, Sydney.
7. Some commentators referred to it as the Fannie Bay aerodrome. These details are from Ross Smith's account sent to the Air Ministry in London.
8. The Australian General Monash was the mastermind behind the successful surprise attack by 400 tanks on the German front line at Amiens on 8 August 1918, afterwards known as 'the black day of the German Army in the history of the war'. Four days later King George V came over to France and knighted him.
9. Personal correspondence with Borton's neighbour Roy Buss.

Bibliography

Antonius, George, *The Arab Awakening*. Hamish Hamilton, 1938.

Armitage, Michael, *The Royal Air Force*. Arms and Armour Press, 1993.

Ash, Eric, *Sir Frederick Sykes and the Air Revolution*. Frank Cass, 1999.

Aspley, T.J. and Wright, Peter 'Blazing the Trail'. Cross & Cockade, Vol. 20, No. 2, 1999.

Baker, Anne, *From Biplane to Spitfire, The Life of Air Chief Marshal Sir Geoffrey Salmond KCB KCMG DSO*. Pen and Sword, 2003.

Banks, Arthur, *A Military Atlas of the First World War*. Heinemann, 1975.

Barr, James, *Setting the Desert on Fire*. Bloomsbury, 2006.

Beevor, Anthony, *Crete. The Battle and the Resistance*. Penguin, 1991.

Bower, Tom, *The Perfect English Spy*. St Martin's Press, 1995.

Bowyer, Chaz, *Handley Page Bombers of World War 1*. Aston Publications Ltd, 1992.

Boyle, Andrew, *Trenchard*. Collins, 1962.

Bruce, Anthony, *The Last Crusade*. John Murray, 2001.

Dowsett, Alan, *Handley Page*. Tempus, 1999.

Egremont, Max, *A Life of Arthur James Balfour*. Collins, 1980.

Eustis, Nelson, *The England to Australia Air Race*. Rigby, 1977.

Garnett, David (Ed.) *The Letters of T.E. Lawrence*. Spring Books, 1964.

Lloyd George, David, *War Memoirs of David Lloyd George* (Vol 1, p. 349). London, Odham, 1938.

BIBLIOGRAPHY

Gilbert, Martin, *Churchill and the Jews*. Simon & Schuster, 2007.

Graves, Robert, *T.E. Lawrence to his Biographer, Robert Graves*. Faber, 1938.

Grigg, John, *Lloyd George War Leader 1916–1918*. Allen Lane, 2002.

Groves, Brigadier P.R.C., *Behind the Smokescreen*. Faber and Faber, 1934.

Hamlin, John, *Always Prepared. The story of 207 Squadron*. RAF. Air Britain Historians Ltd, 1999.

Jenkins, Roy, *Churchill*. MacMillan, 2001

Kerr, Admiral Sir Mark, *Land, Sea and Air*. Longmans, 1927.

Jane's Fighting Aircraft of World War 1. Jane's Publishing Co., 1919.

Laffin, John, *Swifter Than Eagles, The Life of Marshal of the Royal Air Force Sir John Salmond GCB CMG CVO DSO*. Blackwood, 1964.

Lawrence, T.E., *Seven Pillars Of Wisdom*. Jonathan Cape, 1935.

Leslie, Shane, *Mark Sykes. His Life and Letters*. Cassell, 1923.

McMahon, Sir Henry, *Correspondence between Sir Henry McMahon and the Emir Sherif Hussein of Mecca*. HMSO, Cmd 5957, 1939.

MacMillan, Margaret, *Peacemakers*. John Murray, 2001.

Nicolson, Harold, *Peacemaking 1919*. Constable, 1933.

Philby, Rufina, *The Private Life of Kim Philby*. St Ermin's Press, 1999.

Raleigh, Walter and Jones, H.A., *The War in the Air*. Vol. 3, Clarendon Press, 1922–1937.

Semple, Clive, *Diary of a Night Bomber Pilot in WW1*. History Press, 2008.

Slater, Guy, *My Warrior Sons, The Borton Family Diary*. Peter Davies Ltd, 1973.

Smith KBE MC DFC AFC, Sir Ross, *The First Aeroplane Voyage From England to Australia*. Angus and Robertson, 1920.

Soames, Mary, *Clementine Churchill*. Cassell, 1979.

Sykes, Sir Frederick, *From Many Angles*. Harrap, 1942.

Taylor, A.J.P., *English History 1914–1945*. Oxford University Press, 1965.

Taylor, J.W.R., *Pictorial History of the RAF. 1918–1939*. Ian Allen, 1968.

Treadwell, Terry C. and Wood, Alan C., *The First Air War. 1914–1919*. Brasseys UK Ltd, 1996.

Wilson, Jeremy, *The Authorised Biography of T.E. Lawrence*. Heinemann, 1989.

Index